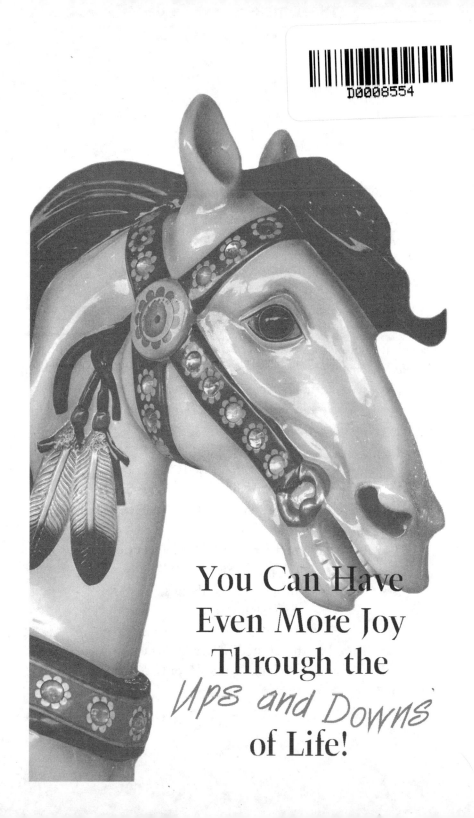

You Can Have
Even More Joy
Through the
Ups and Downs
of Life!

All Scriptures quoted in this volume
are from the King James Bible.

*Though we have checked details of these stories, we know that there
could be some slight discrepancies. We, therefore, ask the mercy
of any reader who may have more knowledge than we do
about any of these stories. Thank you.*

BACK COVER PHOTO
Courtesy of Larry Titak Photography
Schererville, Indiana

Cover Designed for Us by Our Dear Friend,
Ed Russ
Faith Music Ministries
Evansville, Indiana

Printed in the United States of America by
Dickinson Press Inc., Grand Rapids, Michigan

You Can Have Even More Joy Through the Ups and Downs of Life!

JoJo Moffitt

OTHER BOOKS BY JOJO MOFFITT

You Can Have Joy
Through the Ups and Downs of Life

You Can Have More Joy
Through the Ups and Downs of Life

Dedication

It is my privilege and joy to take this opportunity to dedicate the writing of my new book to my precious friend, Mrs. Cathy Berry. She is the wife of Pastor Gary Berry of the Liberty Baptist Church in Charlotte, North Carolina, where they have served together for the past 30 years. She also is the mother of three dear sons and one "darling" granddaughter.

Cathy Berry

Cathy is a precious Christian lady and a tremendous example of one who truly cares for others. She is so kind, caring, and wise, and truly possesses joy in life through the sunshine and the rain.

I love her contagious, upbeat spirit, her sharp sense of humor, and the way she radiates joy, especially on the cloudy days in life.

Thank you, Cathy Berry, for being a living example to me and countless others on how you can have even more joy through the ups and downs of life!

A Gift of Words
to Cathy Berry

It is a great pleasure to be asked to write this article in this encouraging book, *You Can Have Even More Joy Through the Ups and Downs of Life.*

The author of this book has been a tremendous influence in my family's life for over 30 years. JoJo, thanks for the great privilege to be able to express my love and respect to the lady to whom this book is dedicated, my wife, Mrs. Cathy Berry.

I was saved in July 1968 at Faith Baptist Church in Charlotte, North Carolina. Shortly after receiving Christ, I met **Miss Cathy King** (her family attended Faith Baptist Church), who later became the lady we all know as **Mrs. Cathy Berry.**

I knew that there was something *different* about her from the beginning of our relationship. *Every day* she was the *same* person, and **now** after knowing her for over 39 years and being married to her for over 35 years, she has been steadfast and unmoveable in her love for the Lord and His people.

We have been together through many difficult times, but never once have I questioned her character. Many of you have heard her speak in conferences. The words she speaks, the truths that she gives, and the spirit in which she delivers is the same spirit that she has kept in our home. She has a daily walk with our Saviour, a great prayer life, and is a tremendous student of the Word of God.

I have pastored the same church for 30 years (at the time of this writing). Several times as a pastor I have wanted to quit, as most pastors have. I have stayed in the will of God through the encouragement of my helpmeet.

At the time of this writing, I'm home with a broken leg from a fall two weeks ago. Mrs. Berry has been by my side every hour. She is my wife, my best friend, a great mother, and the greatest Christian that I know. My love grows more for her each day. She is truly *the* Proverbs 31 Lady.

– *Dr. Gary Berry*

The Gary Berry Family

My Mother
by Timothy Berry

Describing your mother can go only one of two ways! The first and most popular with Southern boys ends with moist eyes, a Kleenex, and talk of sainthood. The second is good for several trips to a therapist and a prescription for anti-depressants. I would like to pioneer a path indicative and worthy of the woman I call "Mama"! Translating this woman into a vivid and accurate character is not as hard as you might think. Let's see if this is clear. She's Martha Stewart without the jail time; Lucille Ball in the middle of yet another caper, complete with sidekick and yelling husband (you got some 'splaining to do); Judge Judy, with a much bigger gavel; and you think Cinderella had some jealous sisters. She is Wonder Woman without the lasso, but definitely with more clothes (including jewelry! tiara optional).

You might not have noticed Mama's beautiful blue eyes. She can stop all manner of evil and wrongdoing with those. She has brought peace, tranquility, and near heart-failure with a mere glance across a church pew. However, her greatest super-mom-power would have to be her knees!

Several years ago during a particularly difficult family crisis, with me as the villain in this story, I stopped by Mama's house. Bursting through the unlocked door, I ran upstairs, peeking through several doors and was unable to locate her. I knew she was there. There was no faint odor of Tiffany perfume alerting me that she had perfumed herself before leaving the "hall of justice." Where could she be? She needed to hear my problem…I was being victimized, yet again! (excuse the melodrama!)

Then I heard a faint mutter coming from downstairs. I descended the stairs with a whoosh! There she was, on her knees, tears streaming down her face as she begged God's mercy for me!

The sound of her tearful request, pleading my case—I will always remember her crumpled, heaving form as she transformed from ordinary wife, mother, lunch packer, laundry folder, into a Wonder (ful) Woman…..costumed in prayer and tears. She is beautiful, talented, graceful, and poised; but most of all, I'm glad that even though she can't stop bullets, she knows how to quench a fiery dart and halt a roaring lion! That's my wonder-full-of-God Mama!

The Friend of a Friend
by Ben Berry

I met Jesus Christ as Saviour at the age of five, but it was eleven years later that I met Him again in a whole new way. Being 16 years old, my thoughts were naturally on getting my driver's license and a car. I was moping around the house one early spring afternoon. My mother, seeing the wistful look on my face, said "What's wrong, Honey?"

"I'm never going to get a car," I replied.

She then responded with a question that would come to change my life. "Have you prayed about it?"

"Pray about it!?" I thought. "Why would God care if I have a car? It's not like it's a church bus or something."

When I confessed that I hadn't, my mom said, "Well, let's pray about it right now."

My mother took my hand and knelt down with me by the couch in our living room. She touched God that day with the kind of love and concern that can only be given by a mother. I was amazed as she wept over the desires of her son, and I began to see the parallels between my mother and I and the Heavenly Father and His Son. It was on that day that I met Jesus Christ as not just a Saviour, but also as my very best Friend. I guess you could say He was a Friend of a friend.

In case you're wondering, I did get a car. It was a 1966 Volkswagen Beetle that my father and I spent about a year and a half restoring as a project together. We became great friends as well. The car has long since been sold, but the memory of that afternoon prayer will be with me forever.

What I Have Learned From My Mom
by Matthew Berry

Hi, my name is Matthew Berry, and I am the third and the youngest son of Mrs. Cathy Berry. I feel honored that Mrs. Moffitt would give me the pleasure to write a short chapter about my mom. What have I learned from Mom? When life pushes you to a point that you cannot go any farther and when you feel that no one else loves you or even cares about you and when you sadly decide that you want to give yourself a pity party (even though you will be alone there since others possibly may be having a pity party also), you must take one more step forward not looking back at the past but toward the goal that lies ahead. I have seen this in my mom.

I have seen her go onward trying to care for others and not resting for days like she did when her own mother, Mrs. Lucille King, passed away from a heart attack. I also saw as she moved in with her father, the late Rev. Carl King Jr., and willingly took upon herself the position of being his personal nurse until he passed away several months later with colon cancer.

I have not only seen in her a determination to press onward, but I have seen in her an unconditional love that she has shown over and over again for her family, her friends, and for her church. I have seen her show her love for others by taking many hours out of her busy schedule for counseling others by phone and in person, cooking dinner for them, and caring for others through prayer. My mom is no doubt a lady that could have thrown in the towel but has pressed on and has found joy in life even when life did not play fair and when loving others caused her pain and sorrow.

My Friend
by Beth Holtsclaw

Cathy Berry and
Beth Hotsclaw

There are times in our lives when we can't believe the good for ourselves. It is so important to have friends that can believe for you. Mark 2:5 says, *"When Jesus saw their faith, He said to the sick of the palsy, Son, thy sins be forgiven thee."* This sick man had four great friends. Jesus saw their faith. You need to have friends that will help you to see what Jesus can do for you, too!

My friend, Mrs. Cathy Berry, believed the Lord would send a very special man to my life. At almost 40, I could not see that for myself. She kept saying, "Don't give up, but don't give in. The Lord has a plan for your life." My pastor, Dr. Gary Berry, also preached many messages on living for the Lord Jesus. They continued to encourage me, not for months, but for nearly 20 years. And yes, they believed.

One summer we had the privilege of having Dr. Jack Hyles come to our church. He preached a great message about faith. I remember him saying something like, "Shake the dust off of that old prayer request you had but have quit praying about, and start praying about it again." By faith I "dusted off" that prayer about a wonderful husband, one who would love the Lord and love me, and also I asked the Lord for a very tall man.

A few months later a very distinguished gentleman came to our church. He later joined our church. After several conversations I began to notice that he was quiet, kind, and well-established. He, too, had never been married, and he was 6' 5"! We started dating, and he asked me to marry him—I at 40, he at 46! We had the most beautiful wedding, and for 13 years now continue to live "happily ever after."

Mrs. Berry is a wonderful friend and has been a great example of caring and giving. And, oh yes, and of believing!

Acknowledgments

Roy Moffitt, my husband, encouraged me 100% to write this new book. He also gave so sacrificially to help care for all the monetary needs to prepare and publish the materials. Thank you, Roy, for not only being my precious husband of 42½ years, but also for being my buddy, sweetheart, and best friend. I love you, Roy, from the bottom of my heart.

Roy Moffitt,
my sweetheart

Our children—Tina; Roy, Jr.; Mike and his wife Ann Marie; Jason and his wife Allison; Justin and his wife Emily; and, of course, our baby girl, Joy—I love each of you and our priceless grandchildren: Brooke, Brandon, Bryce, Jada, Aidan, and "baby on the way" (due to be born to Mike and Ann Marie in December 2007). A special thanks to Joy, who is normally here at this time and "jumps in" to do extra chores and run errands for me. This summer she is traveling for nine weeks with a tour group from Hyles-Anderson College, singing with the Joyful Melodies singing group. She still encourages me when she calls home each day to "check on me" and "challenge me" with the completion. Thank you, Joy, for being such a great daughter and cheerleader. You all truly are the joys in the life of Dad and me. Please feel the heart of love of a mom that can never be truly expressed in words. I love you; I love you; I love you! So many of these stories are precious memories of the "Moffitt Clan."

The Moffitt Family

Ed and Debbie Russ, the dearest of friends, who actually seem more like family. Ed (or "Mr. Ed" as I refer to him) designed all of my three book covers and also came up with the new title of this book. They also push forward and do the same for anyone who comes into their path. They are brilliant, talented musicians with hearts of gold in giving and serving

Ed and Debbie Russ

others. The Moffitt family truly loves all the Russ family, for sure. Thank you from the bottom of my heart for loving our family and showing it in thought and deed. Thank you, thank you, thank you!

Kim Marsack, my friend and typist, who "did the job above the call of duty." Kim always came in upbeat, high-spirited, and wanting to get the materials typed and completed in a first-class manner. Thanks, Kim, for being such a tremendous blessing and encouragement to me. Thank you for the many times you or your husband Jeff willingly came to my home to pick up new material and even take them to Julie Richter, if needed, to

The Jeff Marsack family

be proofed. I love you and appreciate you, Kim, your wonderful husband Jeff, and your precious girls, Mylee and Cassidy.

Julie Richter

Julie Richter, my friend, who has one of the greatest and most caring spirits. Thank you, Julie, for being so precise and professional in proofing the entire manuscript. I love your helpful spirit. Thank you again for your time and tender heart.

Linda Stubblefield, my longtime friend and fellow worker who worked so hard and late into the night to be sure we had a first-class book. Your typesetting abilities and expertise in

David and Linda Stubblefield

your field have been such a blessing to so many writers and authors. Thank you, Linda, for making my dreams become reality.

Janet Moore, my dear friend, who called often to "cheer me on" and also took her time to make several gallons of my favorite summertime treat, sweet sun tea, and personally deliver it to our home. I love you, Janet, in a special way, and your priceless family, Ron, Tiffany, Crystal, and Meaghan.

The Moore Family

Table of Contents

**Part II — Stories That Bring Even More Joy
Through the Ups and Downs of Life 123**

Table of Contents

You Can Have Even More Joy Through the Ups and Downs of Life!

Preface

You Can Have Even More Joy
Through the Ups and Downs of Life

Thank you, dear friends, David and Linda Stubblefield. The idea of the carousel should be credited to our good friends and coworkers, David and Linda Stubblefield. One day while they were driving, they came up with the idea of how a carousel or merry-go-round represented the lives of the Moffitts. I could not help but agree with them, and I wanted to give them a special acknowledgment for helping set the foundation of this book. You see, one of the most exciting, amazing, and colorful rides I remember as a child was the carousel or, as I also called it, the merry-go-round.

I remember how I was fascinated with the colored lights, festive music, and decorative horses. I never was drawn to the stationary horses; they just seemed dull and presented no challenge. After all, they never did anything—they just sat still. I was mesmerized by the horses that moved—the ones that went up and down. To me, they were the ones that represented life.

Life can be exciting, fun, and challenging; yet a person can get scared, apprehensive, and even get physically sick. Still, we need to keep on keeping on until the end of the ride. Yes, life has its ups and downs, but more important is how a person looks at life.

"All the days of the afflicted are evil: but he that is of a merry heart hath a continual feast." (Proverbs 15:15) I trust these stories of true-to-life teachings might help those who read these pages to see how life does have its down times, but through humor we can turn the down times around. Yes, life should be like a merry-go-round with its ups and downs, its triumphs and tragedies, its joys and sorrows.

"To every thing there is a season, and a time to every purpose under the heaven: A time to be born, and a time to die; a time to plant, and a time to pluck up that which is planted; A time to kill, and a time to heal; a time to break down, and a time to build up; A time to weep, and a time to laugh; a time to mourn, and a time to dance; A time to cast away stones, and time to gather stones together; a time to embrace, and a time to refrain from embracing; A time to get, and a time to lose; a time to keep, and a time to cast away; A time to rend, and a time to sew; a time to keep silence, and a time to speak; A time to love, and a time to hate; a time of war, and a time of peace." (Ecclesiastes 3:1-8)

The Stubblefield Family
Standing:
David and Linda
Melissa and her husband,
Brandon Dillard
Seated:
Hugh and Bethany
McCraney
Linda's father,
Gordon Alexander

Introduction
by Dr. Jack Schaap

My Preacher

F ew Christians succeed through prosperity. Christianity is a religion that thrives on adversity. In fact, those Christians whom we usually admire most are those who have struggled to overcome one or more hardships, or they are those who spend their lives helping those who live in adversity.

Roy and JoJo Moffitt are such people. Roy and JoJo are transparent. The face of love and joy reflects a pure and sincere heart. Roy and JoJo are tested. Their trials and adversities have been many and difficult; yet, their faith and zeal are genuine and contagious.

JoJo has put to words in this book the cadence and rhythm of hers and Roy's life, living with and for those struggling with adversity. Here you will find again the tempo of Christianity lived on the edge of desperation yet filled with joy unspeakable and full of glory.

How pleased I am to pastor and to work with real Christian heroes like Roy and JoJo Moffitt. How happy I am to recommend the author and her book!

Pastor and Mrs. Jack Schaap
First Baptist Church
Hammond, Indiana

Foreword
by Cindy Schaap

I t was my privilege to write an introduction for Mrs. Moffitt's last book. Since that time I have been privileged to get to know the author even better. I believe in her as much as I ever have. JoJo and I have been blessed to speak at several ladies' conferences together as well as to travel together. I am always refreshed when I hear that Mrs. Moffitt will be one of the speakers with whom I will be speaking at a conference. I know that when Mrs. Moffitt is around, the atmosphere will remain positive.

Cindy Schaap, my preacher's wife

Every word she speaks in my presence is an uplifting word.

I am aware that Mrs. Moffitt has suffered several types of rejection in her life, and I am in awe of her great spirit that she manifests in spite of, not only these heartaches, but also serious health problems. I highly recommend the author, JoJo Moffitt. She is a qualified author for the subject of this book.

I also recommend her highly as a church member and as a personal friend. I am honored to be her coworker, her pastor's wife, and her friend.

Meet More of My Family...

Above: "The Moffitt Girls"
Left to right: Emily, JoJo, Allison, Joy, Ann Marie

Below: Spring break in Gatlinburg, Tennessee, 2007
Left to right: Justin; Emily; JoJo; Roy, Sr.; Roy, Jr.

Introductory Remarks
by Dr. Roy Moffitt

To know JoJo Moffitt is to love JoJo Moffitt. JoJo has a way of entering one's life as soon as she meets that person. No one is a stranger to her. She has a divine gift from God to bring joy to people's lives just because they get to meet her. JoJo has a compassionate heart that

My honey and me!

reaches out to everyone she meets. A person can be going through a very tough time in his life but feel much better because he met JoJo Moffitt. She has a unique way of leaving her life and entering your world. We have been married since 1965, and JoJo never ceases to amaze me in how much she can accomplish in one day.

The writing of this book took a lot of time and preparation, but in the process of all the time spent writing this book, she still made time for all the important duties she has in her life. She taught her summer school class; she made time to visit her bus route, rode her bus on Sunday, and helped out in my adult Sunday school class, greeting people and making them feel welcome on Sunday morning. She always has a dinner prepared for her family. You will never walk into our home and find the house messy, dirty dishes in the sink, beds unmade, or the floors dirty. I have said for many years that you can come over any time to visit us, and you do not have to have to give us a warning before you come over.

JoJo has a unique way of turning tough times into victories. That's why she has done such a good job in writing her books. They deal with the tough times of life, but somehow they seem to run into victories and blessings.

I am very proud of my wife JoJo. I believe I can say she is very real. To know JoJo is to love JoJo.

Part I—Meet Some of My Greatest Heroes and Friends!

I am honored to introduce you to several heroes in my life who have taught me in word and in deed. They are the folks I pattern my life after and actually look to them as my teachers and friends.

Many of them have gone through unbelievable trials, heartaches, and challenges; and yet they "keep on keeping on." They have never quit but have learned from their life situations and help others to do the same.

I trust they will be a special help, encouragement, and true blessing and joy to you as you read their stories and learn from their lives. I love and admire them more than words can ever express. Meet my heroes and friends.

Turning Your Sorrows Into Even More Joy

by Cathy Berry

"...and sorrow is turned into joy before him." (Job 41:22)

J esus said in John 15:11, *"These things have I spoken unto you, that my joy might remain in you, and that your joy might be full."* I think a lot of times people do not understand joy because they do not understand sorrow. To have joy, you must have sorrow. For there to be light, there has to be darkness; for there to be love, there must be hatred; for there to be honesty, there must be dishonesty. The world and Christian people must experience sorrow so that they can truly experience and understand joy.

When I was eight years old, my family went to the Mecklenburg County Fair. This was a very exciting time for me because we just didn't do those kinds of things. We did not ever have the money to do those kind of things; but this time we did, and my mom, dad, my two older sisters, and I went to the fair! When we got there, my mom and dad had to select the rides that we could ride. We walked through the fair and eventually saw all the different things we could, and we finally got to the merry-go-round (that's what we call a carousel down South).

We were so excited about riding the merry-go-round. When it

was finally our turn to get on, the man in charge of the merry- go-round told us to get on and find a seat. It was such a mixture of fun and fear to get on this merry-go-round. We were trying to choose which horse we wanted to ride. There were so many beautiful horses on the merry-go-round, along with tigers, leopards, and giraffes. There were also sleighs where people could sit and ride and not go up and down. We all chose one, and it started. As you know, it started out very slowly and then progressively got faster and faster as the music got louder and louder. Each time the ride went around, I tried to find my parents standing on the outskirts of the merry-go-round. I remember my sisters were trying to hold hands with each other as their horses would go up and down. Are we having fun yet?

Life is much like riding a merry-go-round because there are so many sorrows that come our way as we go through this life. I have made a list of some of the sorrows that I have experienced.

I remember when my dog passed away. We had her for 13 years. How sorrowful that was. By the way, **dogs do go to Heaven!**

I had a car accident that should have killed me. The accident totaled my car and crushed my knee, even though we did not know it was crushed for six weeks. This meant no more ballroom dancing. (Ha! Ha! Ha!)

- We had church problems which brought lies, gossip, and rumors.
- One of our sons had marital problems.
- One son got divorced—a very sad divorce.
- We had a church split, and with it came more rumors, lies, gossip, and a question of character.

    Have you taken out your Kleenex yet?
- The church finances got into trouble, and then we personally got audited by IRS.

    Now is when you need some chocolate!

- Dr. Hyles passed away. I thought I was just going to die, just as I'm sure many people did.
- My father-in-law passed away.
- My mother-in-law passed away.
- My mom suddenly passed away in 2005. She went into cardiac arrest while she was packing dad's suitcase for Dad to go into the hospital for colon cancer surgery.
- My dad passed away in 2006 with colon cancer.
- And now at present, my husband has a broken leg. We have also had four funerals, and my son had an accident in *my car!* This is all during the same time frame of my husband's broken leg.

We will have sorrow, but that is how we understand what joy is about.

Having the fun of riding a merry-go-round comes with some fear. Isn't it amazing that we pay people to scare us? We condition ourselves through the process of telling ourselves through the years not to be afraid. "Don't be afraid of the merry-go-round. Don't be afraid of these things." That is how we go through life as we condition ourselves that we are going to survive this. We're going to make it through this.

In particular I remember when Brother Hyles passed away. I remember how sad we were when we got the phone call that he had passed away. None of us really expected it; I think we all thought he would live forever. I cried *so hard* for days. At one point in our den on my knees, I said, "Lord, I don't understand. I just don't understand why. Why would You let Brother Hyles come on to Heaven when we need him so badly here?"

A Scripture came to my heart that gave me such clear understanding. In my deep sorrow, this verse came. "*...and death by sin; and so death passed upon all men, for that all have sinned.*" (Romans 5:12) Because of sin in the Garden of Eden, Brother Hyles had to die. For the first time when that thought and that verse crossed my heart and my mind, I sat in the floor of my den, and **I hated sin like I had never before hated sin.** The sin in the Garden of Eden took Brother Hyles to Heaven. When my parents left this world, I understood that it was because of the penalty of sin in the Garden of Eden and the sin of this world. And so, of course, we can't always choose.

Like riding the merry-go-round, we choose our horse or sleigh. A lot of older adults were riding the sleighs because they didn't want the ups and downs. And of course, none of us do either. But they chose the sleighs, and we chose the excitement. Children want the excitement, the ups and downs, so they chose the horses. As we get older in life, we don't want those ups and downs. If we could choose, we would ride a sleigh through life. We would just ride along in our sleigh, wave at everyone, and watch everyone else go through their ups and downs. We would not even be bothered with the hardships and the sadness of this life.

But we don't get to choose. John 15:6 says, *"If a man abide not in me, he is cast forth as a branch, and is withered; and men gather them, and cast them into the fire, and they are burned."*

I think of my sisters trying to hold hands. It would be nice if you could always have somebody to hold your hand when you are going through your ups or your downs. It would be nice if there were somebody to pull you up or if there was somebody to hang onto you when you are down.

The Bible *says, "Trust in the* LORD...." It doesn't say trust in people. It doesn't even say trust in your church. It doesn't say trust in your husband. It doesn't say trust in your finances. It says, *"Trust in the* LORD...." You will have to ride alone on that merry-go-round on that pony. You'll have to ride alone sometimes.

It gets very noisy, and there are a lot of different things on the merry-go round. All the children are screaming and laughing, and there's your own laughter and screaming. There are many different noises on that merry-go-round. In life there are a lot of noises that will take you away from the One Who will help you through your sorrow. You'll have your family—their voices—they will have an opinion. People in your life will have an opinion. There will always be circumstances, your job, and your ministry at church. They all have a voice, but it is that "still small voice" of God to which we have to keep listening. We're going to walk through some hard times. Psalms 23 says that you "*walk through the valley of the shadow of death.*"

You are going to walk through the sorrows of this life. There are different kinds of sorrows that are in this world. There's the *sorrow from the world's system.* The world tries to make you believe that wrong is right and that right is wrong. We live in a world that brings sorrow to you because here is all this wrong and you're thinking, "This is not right," but everyone around you believes that it's okay. We're going to live in that kind of sorrow. It is going to be there around us, and we can't conform to it.

There is **sorrow from other people**. "*These things have I spoken unto you, that my joy might remain in you, and that your joy might be full. This is my commandment, That ye love one another, as I have loved you.*" (John 15:11-12) There are going to be other people who disappoint you, who are unkind, who are inconsiderate of you. The principle to learn is not to get consumed with all the sorrow that they try to put into your life. The Bible says, "*As a man thinketh in his heart, so is he.*" I have learned for myself that if I ponder the sorrows people present to me, if I think about them, if I allow myself to consider those sorrows too much, then I become like them. Proverbs 23:7 says, "*For as he thinketh in his heart, so is he.*"

A good friend of mine said, "You will never understand crazy people. You'll never understand them and why they do what they do. They are going to do what they are going to do." You have to let people do what they're going to do.

"Blessed are ye, when men shall hate you, and when they shall sepa-rate you from their company, and shall reproach you, and cast out your name as evil, for the Son of man's sake. Rejoice ye in that day, and leap for joy: for, behold, your reward is great in heaven: for in the like man-ner did their fathers unto the prophets." (Luke 6:22-23)

You will have **sorrows from your own expectations**. It's amaz-ing sometimes the kinds of expectations we put upon ourselves because we think we should be more, should have done more. "I wish I could look like her. I wish I could teach like her. I wish I could be like her. I wish I had a house like that. I wish I could be a mother like she is. I wish I could have done things like she does them."

We have all these expectations. I think this is one of the great-est lessons I have ever learned, this sorrow of my own expecta-tions. This type of sorrow will take you into a deep, deep despair. It is very important for us to understand why the Lord will allow these great sorrows. You know, I find it very interesting that Jesus was described as a man of sorrows. He knew what sorrow was about. But it is out of that great sorrow that comes great fruitful-ness. So, He will allow you and me to go into great sorrow because He desires great fruitfulness from us. When we go into this great sorrow, we will produce this great fruitfulness.

I remember when our church was very young, and many things were happening in our lives with a lot of struggles. At one point, there was a great hopelessness in my life. I just didn't see things getting any better. I didn't feel like things were ever going to be in my own heart the way that I thought they should be. I knew that my heart was deceitful. But at that point, I couldn't get past my own expectations and that sorrow that was so deep in my heart. I remember thinking, "I just want to go to Heaven." I became consumed with that thought. I didn't want to have to live the life that we were living anymore.

I remember one night while getting ready to go to bed thinking, "Tomorrow is that day." It had been a thought in my heart and mind for a long time, even to the process of planning what I would do. I remember that night, getting ready for bed and looking over at my husband and thinking, "He's going to have a very hard time, and I am very sorry." I went on to sleep. The next morning after getting up, I hadn't spoken a whole lot. I got my boys ready for school, packed their lunches, took them to school, and told them goodbye. As they walked into the school building, they waved, and I told them I loved them, knowing that would be my final goodbye to them.

When I pulled away from the curb and headed toward home, I knew that by midmorning everything would be over, and I would be in Heaven. There was a sense of relief for me. When I got home, I started to prepare some things that I did not want to leave undone. As I did so, the phone rang; it was my oldest son.

"Mom, I left my North Carolina report in my bedroom on the desk."

I said, "Son, can't you take it tomorrow?"

He said, "No, I have to turn it in today."

I tried to offer him other solutions, but he was persistent. He **had** to have it that day. So I agreed to bring it. I picked up his report and drove to the school which was less than ten minutes away. I took the report into the office and told them what my son needed. I was assured they would call him to come and get it.

Let me say here—don't feel guilty if you do not know that a person is planning suicide. A person who is going to commit suicide truly does not want anyone to know. The person is so self-absorbed that it's where he would not want anyone to stop him. A person who does let on or does make you aware is asking you to stop him. Be sensitive to that because the risk is there, but he wants you to stop him. A person who does not want to be stopped does not ever let on. I'm saying this from my own personal experience. You would never know. The person will go through the motions of all the things that he normally does because he does not want anyone to stop him.

As I drove toward home, a still, small voice said, "You need to go by a particular young lady's house and tell her that you love her before you go do this because she is a young Christian. She's not going to recover from this very well. You just need to go and tell her you love her."

So I did. To this day I know that it was just that still, small voice of God speaking to me and helping me. Her house was not far out of the way, so I went by. The Holy Spirit knew she would not be home, but I wrote her a note. I did not understand it at that point, but I understood it later. I wrote a note that said, "I want you to know that I will always love you no matter what," and I put that note into the window pane of her front door. (I still did not understand, but the Lord was teaching me a deep, deep truth.) Many years later I told her about my visit to her house, and I learned that the note had blown off of her door and had blown away! Thank You, Jesus!!

As I left her house, that same still, small voice spoke again and said, "You need to go by and check on another couple before you do this because they, too, are young Christians and will not understand and will have a very difficult recovery. You must go by first." So, I did!

I went by, not thinking about myself at this point, but caring about someone else—I hope you are getting this now. I knocked on the door of this young couple and could hear the children. Eventually, the young mother came and opened the door. I could see that she was in distress. I greeted her with a kind, "Hello."

She said, "Mrs. Berry! The Lord sent you by here!"

Inside I was thinking, "Girl, you are a mess!" *"For as he thin-keth in his heart, so is he: Eat and drink, saith he to thee; but his heart is not with thee."* (Proverbs 23:7)

She began to weep and hugged me. She took me into her very disheveled home. The children were disheveled, and she was disheveled.

I sat down with her, and even in my own sorrow, I listened to her sorrows and thought, "Everything that she is saying is only a thimble compared to my reservoir of sorrow." Yet I continued to listen until she was finished.

I said, "Let me help you." I gathered the children and put them in the tub. I then went to her room and laid her on the bed, covered her, and stroked her hair as she cried and then drifted off to sleep. I dressed and fed the children and put them at play. I set about to clean her house.

She woke early in the afternoon, and we had some tea, talked some more, and I showed her some Scriptures. She said, "It's about time for my husband to get home, and I don't know if you want to be here when he gets home."

I said, "Oh yes, I most certainly do want to be here. Let's cook him a nice supper, and while it is cooking, why don't you go take a shower, get dressed, and be all pretty. The house is straightened up, the beds are made, and the children are playing and content."

I finished cooking supper, washing dishes as I went so she would not have much with which to deal later. I set the table and went out in her yard and picked some flowers for the table. Everything was done when she came in. Just a few minutes later, we heard his truck pull in. She looked at me sort of anxiously. I told her that everything was going to be fine. (I had a frying pan or a prayer, whichever we needed!)

He came in and was surprised that I was there. I greeted him,

"Hello! How are you?" He looked around. All the clothes were folded, the dishes were done, the floors were clean, the children looked good, and his wife looked very pretty. Everyone's spirit was okay, well, pretty much everybody's spirit.

I told them it was time for me to go. I told them I loved their family, but I had to go cook supper for my husband and sons. As she walked me to the door, she said, "Mrs. Berry, you have saved me today."

I hugged her deeply and said, "No, you have saved me." She looked at me, bewildered, but I knew in my heart what I had already planned for that day.

God is so amazing in the way that He works in our lives when we are His children. When He has the freedom to work and we listen to that still, small voice, it is amazing what He will accomplish in our lives. He will take us through some very hurtful things so that we can be fruitful. After that time in my life, it was like what the Apostle Paul said in Philippians 4:11, *"...for I have learned, in whatsoever state I am, therewith to be content."* He was saying that he had learned *to just have joy—no matter what.*

As I drove home that afternoon, I learned that my joy in my expectations was going to have to be for other people. I could not consume myself with myself. I could not worry about my own expectations; I had to be consumed with others. Down the road when hard times came—and they have come many, many times—I have had to go to dwell on how others are feeling and not on how I am feeling. That is why Paul said, *"I know how both how to be abased, and I know how to abound: every where and in all things I am instructed both to be full and to be hungry, both to abound and to* ***suffer need.****"* (Philippians 4:12) Paul said that he still had his joy.

I still have my joy! Your own expectations will bring you a lot of sorrow. You have to care about other people. Brother Hyles used to say, "Others, Lord, yes, others. Let this my motto be. Help me to live for others that I may live like Thee." It was one of the greatest sermons that I heard as a young Christian, but the truth of it came for me in that deep sorrow. It was after that that I did not have such a judgmental attitude toward myself. *I got over myself.* The Lord allowed that affliction so that I would gain a lot of knowledge and judgment about myself so that I would be more fruitful. That's what I Corinthians 11:31 says, *"For if we would judge ourselves, we should not be judged."* We should use those times of deep sorrow and despair to judge ourselves so that we can get past ourselves to serve other people.

Jesus did. I Timothy 6:10 says that He was pierced with many sorrows. He cared very much for people and took on their sorrows. When I go through hard times, I have learned to ask God, "What are You trying to teach me?" instead of, "What am I doing wrong?" I'm not good enough. I'm not good enough to sing. I'm not good enough to teach, soul win, be a pastor's wife, Christian, mother. I am not good at anything.

It was getting past all those "self" things that caused me to be more fruitful. Why is it always all about you? It could be your turn to live what *you say* you believe!

The Bible calls another sorrow the *sorrow of those who have no hope.* My mom was one of the greatest ladies I have ever known. She had such a kind and caring heart for people. She loved my dad and helped him be and do whatever he desired. That is the way she lived, and I believe that God let her die that same way…taking care of others. I think of her packing his suitcase to go into surgery for colon cancer that he would most likely not have survived. My mom had been telling us for months that he needed the surgery but would not be here much longer. We all felt like he would die soon. She packed his suitcase and went into cardiac arrest caring for him.

My dad said about my mother, "Cathy, for 55 years your mother has given me no grief, no sorrow." Isn't that what the Proverbs 31 lady is about? *"She will do him good and not evil all the days of her life."* (v. 12) That is what my mom did. My dad did not even know how to make coffee! He didn't even know what he liked to eat! My mom cooked it, and he ate it. He was a man's man who liked to fish, hunt, and play sports. It was just that she took such good care of him that he didn't even know what he liked. She laid out all his clothes for him. He never had to worry. He could match things up, but he never had to think about that sort of thing. She loved him more than anything and wanted to serve him.

There was such great sorrow for my dad when Mom went to Heaven. He missed her so badly. Every day we put her pictures around him in those last months that he lived. He would say, "Cathy, your momma is smiling at me. Cathy, your momma is winking at me." He missed her so dearly, and he longed to see her again. Then, when he passed away, there was great sorrow. I had asked the Lord and even asked several people to pray with me that I would see my dad when he saw my mom for the first time in Heaven. It seemed like a strange request, but I wanted them to be together because he had missed her so badly. She had so dreaded this surgery for him, his final months and days, not having any idea that she would be in Heaven first. I often thought that she was there first getting everything ready for him once again. I am sure that she did because that is the kind of woman that she was.

My dad was very alert even up to the last minutes of his life here on earth. I was trying to care for him around the clock. My husband had gone to get us something to eat. My dad had curled up a little bit. The hospice nurse had told me to watch his breathing move from his abdomen, to his chest, to his throat. We watched his breathing change, and as it did, he began to whisper. I thought he was whispering to me, so I got down close to him. He was not whispering to me. It was like he was not even in this world. I could not even tell what he was saying. I thought that if he were talking to someone else, it was not any of my business, so I backed away. He was still whispering. I noticed that his feet had begun to move like he may be walking. His eyes began to glisten. He began to talk with this person that we did not see. His face showed such love for this person. It was almost romantic. His face looked young again. He was not on any strong medications or oxygen or a morphine pump, as many cancer patients are. He only took a mild pain medication. He was just in another world. I truly believe that he was talking to my mom. I believe that my mother came and said, "Come on, Junior; let's go." That's what she had always done. If they were at church, a restaurant, or my home, she would always be the one to say, "Come on, Junior; let's go." I believe the Lord let her come to get him.

You know, I don't sorrow as others who have no hope because I know that there will be an end to my ride on this merry-go-round of life. These hard times will pass. Every one of them has passed. All along the way they have all passed.

Jesus said in John 16:20, *"Verily, verily, I say unto you, That ye shall weep and lament, but the world shall rejoice: and ye shall be sorrowful, but your sorrow shall be turned into joy."* He was talking with them about His going to the Cross. He said, "Your sorrows will be turned into joy because this ride will be over and it will pass." The tribulations, the sorrow, the sickness, and the misunderstandings will be over. All the things of this life will pass—just like the man who runs the merry-go-round said, "All right, the ride is over. I hope you had a great time and that you will ride again."

You know we need to keep our eye on the joy of the Lord—the joy of Heaven. Don't get so involved in the things of this world or involved in yourselves so much because the Lord has a joy for us now. I Thessalonians 5:16 says, *"Rejoice evermore."* We can do this if we rejoice on things that are eternal: Jesus, the Word of God, our church, God's love for us, our home in Heaven, the love God gives us for other people, our family here and in Heaven, the lessons God has taught us, the people who have loved us, kind words and deeds, and God's gracious forgiveness and mercy.

I long to hear God say, *"Well done, thou good and faithful servant."* I hope that you will *choose* to have even more joy on your merry-go-round because it will bring you even more joy in the ups and downs of life.

The Bible says that someday Jesus will say, *"...enter thou into the joy of thy lord."* (Matthew 25:21) He **could** be saying that in Heaven there is only joy. Hallelujah for that!

But until then, there will be ups and downs on the merry-go-round, and you can have even more joy. "Get your ticket, please."

Joy—Passing It On

by Ed Russ

Having joy is very important to every child of God. It is especially important for the Christian because it has a tremendous effect on the lives of people around him. Nehemiah said *"...neither be ye sorry; for the joy of the LORD is your strength."* This joy is passed down to us from the Lord, and we can pass it on to others. It is the joy of the Lord that sustains us and helps us to become what we should be for the Lord.

I have been privileged to work with music my entire ministry. Music is one of those things that is passed on from person to person because it brings enjoyment. But enjoyment should not be the goal. Since music was created for God first and man second, the goal should be to honor God. When we honor God first, then God passes joy on to us. So God passes joy on to His children; and when they possess joy, the effects of it are passed on to those around them. However, when a person escapes through music, the end result is self-satisfaction. When we satisfy the flesh first and merely try to include God, depression is the result and not joy.

Since we all prefer joy over sorrow and happiness over sadness, let me suggest a few things that will help us to pass on the joy of the Lord. Ephesians 5:19-21 gives us a formula that can't lose!

1. **Music people should be happy!** *"Speaking to yourselves in psalms and hymns and spiritual songs, singing and making melody in your heart to the Lord."* (Ephesians 5:19)

The music you choose should also bring about and promote joy and happiness. I am sure that we have all been exposed to music that has a negative message, but we do not have to make it a regular part of our music diet. I often encourage people to be careful about an overabundance of music that talks about their personal experience. That kind of music tends to be selfish. In a lot of the new modern music, the melody is not the main thing. We need to make melody in our hearts. If melody is in your heart, you cannot help but pass along a little joy.

2. **Music people are thankful people!** *"Giving thanks always for all things unto God and the Father in the name of our Lord Jesus Christ."* (Ephesians 5:20)

Have you ever heard of the temperamental musician? That is the musician who is only interested in his performance, rather than the listener's enjoyment. Those people are usually not thankful. When we find many different ways to express gratitude, we tend to have a lot of friends. When we have a lot of friends, we tend to pass joy around.

3. **Music people should be submitted people!** *"Submitting yourselves one to another in the fear of God."* (Ephesians 5:21)

Find a person who understands authority, and you will find a person that does not have any trouble coming under authority. Give God your music, and He will give you joy in return. This should be the goal of each and every one of us.

The Russ Family
Left to right: Bobbie, Ryan, Adam, Ed, Debbie,
Stephen, and David

With Hearts Full of Love
and Gratitude to the Russ Family
from the Moffitts

Thank you from the bottom of our hearts for being "sold out" to serve the Lord and to serve His people, which includes our family.

Thank you for loving the Lord with your whole heart, soul, body, and mind, and for teaching us how we, too, can do the same.

Thank you for never being satisfied but constantly striving to go forward and grow.

Thank you for never quitting, especially when the battles arise, but continuing to fight on and turn near defeats into victory.

You Can Have Even More Joy Through the Ups and Downs of Life!

Please feel the love, respect, gratitude, and admiration of the Roy Moffitt family. We love you both and your family dearly. Thank you from the bottom of our hearts.

Fiery Trials

by Dr. Wendell Evans

"Beloved, think it not strange concerning the fiery trial which is to try you, as though some strange thing happened unto you." (I Peter 4:12)

My friends,
Dr. and Mrs. Wendell Evans

Are you going through a trial so severe that it seems to be a "fiery trial"? Most of us have had such an experience. When you are in your seventies, friends and associates love to tease you about your age.

One of my students asked, "Dr. Evans, did you hear Abraham Lincoln give his Gettysburg address?"

I said, "No, but I did hear George Washington give his second inaugural."

I griped about the Chicago Cubs' absence from the World Series for 100 years. Dr. Ray Young, my good friend and co-president, said, "Brother Evans, did you get to see any of those games?"

I said, "Yes, and it was a long buggy ride from Iowa to Chicago, too."

The point is, if you are very old, you have probably been through the wringer a few times. My first wife Marlene suffered with cancer off and on for about 18 years. She only cried to me about it once! I think she handled that cancer pretty well, thanks to the prayers of thousands of believers.

My wife Elaine was left alone to care for three younger siblings when she was six years of age. After growing up in an orphanage where she was reared by nuns and priests, she was sometimes homeless. She had a severe illness and therefore could not obtain a job. Elaine had to have a large goiter removed at 23 years of age. She had doubts about the ritualistic religion of her childhood, but she clung to God in prayer. She lost two husbands to death in three and one-half years. Two years after she got saved, her husband Jimmy was found to have cancer throughout his body. She felt that the trial was too fiery.

In the midst of one of her worst days, Marlene Evans called. Elaine told Marlene that she was going to quit church as soon as Jimmy went to Heaven. Marlene said, "You are going through a bad time, but you will be all right, and you will not leave church."

Elaine said, "Don't tell me what I will do!"

Thanks to Marlene and a fine Christian lady named Rosalla Fletcher, Elaine did not leave church.

The moral of the story is that if a couple of people take time to care about the one who is in the "fire," he or she can make it! Is there someone you could help today?

In the days when the early Christians read I Peter 4:12, the verse had a dramatic meaning! God' people were being flogged, beaten, imprisoned, and sometimes killed. Paul tells about his fiery trials in II Corinthians 11:24 and 25, *"Of the Jews five times received I forty stripes save one. Thrice was I beaten with rods, once was I stoned, thrice I suffered shipwreck, a night and a day I have been in the deep."*

We don't have the same type of "fiery trial" that God's people had in the days of Peter and Paul, but we do have trials. As I write these words, the 29-year-old son of a dear friend lies in a California hospital bed with about 300 screws in his head. He had a terrible motorcycle accident several days ago, and he is fighting for his life. That is no small trial for his parents, Dr. and Mrs. Keith Gomez. It's not a light affliction for the young man or for his brother. I have known these boys since they were little guys. They attended Hyles-Anderson College, and I love them both. I pray for Joshua Gomez and his family many times a day.

Dear friend, you have no idea what may lurk around the next turn in the road of life. I cannot begin to mention the trials that are hounding God's people right now. Just a few hours ago, a dear pastor poured out his heart to me. Just before that, it was a fine missionary. Right here in Indiana, a pastor's daughter is going through a terrible time physically. In Michigan a pastor's grand-daughter is fighting for her health. The family would be elated if this little girl could just stop having seizures. The father of one of my history students has been sick for months. Dr. Bill Burr is a great man if I am a judge of character, but as I write these words, he is fighting a terrible war with cancer. The same is true of a wonderful pastor's wife in Washington State, Mrs. Dorothy Paisley.

A word of warning: sorrows and trials can become anguish if you don't keep your eyes on Jesus!

Meet More of My Friends...

Paul and Edie Boyce and sons, Cullen and Stephen

Don and Linda Boyd

How We Keep Going— 30 Years of Marriage and Counting

by Bill Boyd

"Brethren, I count not myself to have apprehended: but this one thing I do, forgetting those things which are behind, and reaching forth unto those things which are before." (Philippians 3:13)

My wife Cricket and I had been called by God into the ministry, and after graduation from Hyles-Anderson College, we pastored for a few years in Tennessee. We came back to our home in Virginia where there was a desperate need of an independent fundamental Baptist church in the area. We began with a home-made pulpit and some borrowed chairs from a local school. I took a job in the construction field, and Cricket went to work as a secretary/bookkeeper at a real estate office. The church

Bill and Cricket Boyd

was averaging 40 with a high day of 55, but little did we know that on Thursday, February 11, 1999, our whole lives would be changed.

At approximately 3:30 p.m., Cricket received a phone call at her office telling her that I had been in a serious accident at work and that she needed to come to the hospital. Cricket was already so sick and so shaken by the call that she could not drive herself. When she finally arrived at the hospital, she learned that I had been working from a forklift-type machine 30 feet in the air; when I finished with the work, instead of lowering me to the ground, the operator dumped me off, and I fell headfirst on the sidewalk. The fall broke my neck and my back, and my crushed skull exposed my brain. I was in such bad condition that the ER doctors gave me a zero percent chance of living for the first 48 hours.

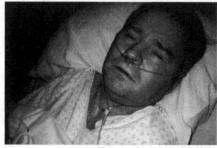

Bill Boyd
————

Through many surgeries and much rehab, the Lord allowed me to come home nine months later, yet I am now confined to a wheelchair as a quadriplegic for the rest of my life. During my stay at home, three doctors who were caring for me were prescribing medications but not keeping track of each other's orders. Because I strictly following their orders, I suffered four drug overdoses, each one putting me into the hospital for a week or more. Because Cricket had videotaped me during the overdoses, when I finally came around, I agreed to go into a nursing home for 30 days to try to get straightened out. After the 30 days, there was another 30, and then another until finally the total ended up being 482 days.

Upon the day of my release, Cricket picked me up and drove all night to St. John, Indiana, where she had purchased a house and had turned it into a universal home for us. The accident happened when I was 40 years old, and I am presently 49. I suffer with severe pain every day of my life, yet I teach part-time at Hyles-

Anderson College and substitute teach for Sunday school at First Baptist Church, Hammond, Indiana, while being cared for by Cricket 24 hours a day. How do we keep going in spite of what has happened to us?

1. PRAYER. We serve a prayer-answering God. We can pray and ask Him for grace and help through anything we experience. Jesus said, *"...behold, Satan hath desired to have you, that he may sift you as wheat: But I have prayed for thee, that thy faith fail not: and when thou art converted, strengthen thy brethren."* (Luke 22:31-32) When the accident first happened, Cricket stayed on the phone to ask men of God like Dr. Tom Williams and preacher and their church families to pray for me. Of course, we are thankful for those faithful families and friends who remember to pray for us every day since then.

2. PREACHING. As I lay there in the second hospital, I could hear Dr. Jack Hyles preaching his sermon, "Knocked Down But Not Knocked Out." Preaching is so vitally important! Sunday morning, Sunday night, and Wednesday night are crucial to us— we need to hear the man of God beyond what we can express in words. My pastor, Dr. Jack Schaap, preached a sermon, "I Choose to Survive," making us realize we can choose to quit or to keep going. Dr. Lee Roberson, Dr. Wendell Evans, Mrs. Marlene Evans, Mrs. JoJo Moffitt, and others encouraged us through their personal lives, messages, and books.

3. PEOPLE. We have many examples from whom we learned. My mom had cancer and when she went in for chemotherapy, she asked them to connect her to an IV with wheels so she could pass out Gospel tracts and witness to the other patients. Brother Hyles, who was severely and continuously attacked by the Devil through people, kept going. Because Cricket stayed with me when most people in this type of situation are abandoned, our love for each other continues to grow. Many people are looking to us as an example, especially our children and grandchildren, who say, "Our mom and dad are not quitters, regardless of what happens to them" (Proverbs 17:6). We would not have crossed the paths of many lost people to whom we have witnessed and others we did lead to Jesus if this accident had not happened. When soul winning, we get to share our testimony of how I almost died and springboard from my testimony into leading them to Jesus, sharing the grace of God with them (II Corinthians 12:9).

    4. PROMISES of GOD. "Standing on the Promises" is more than just a song we sing in church; it is a truth that we can stand on in God's Word! I Corinthians 10:13 says, *"There hath no temptation taken you but such as is common to man: but God is faithful, who will not suffer you to be tempted above that ye are able; but will with the temptation also make a way to escape, that ye may be able to bear it."* Some other promises to stand on are:

- Genesis 28:15
- Proverbs 3:5, 6
- Philippians 4:13
- I Peter 5:7
- Hebrews 13:5
- Romans 8:28, 32, 37
- John 14:1-3
- Matthew 6:33
- Jeremiah 33:3
- Isaiah 26:3
- Job 42:5
- Psalm 23
- Galatians 2:20
- II Corinthians 12:9
- I John 2:28
- Ephesians 3:19, 20
- II Corinthians 1:3, 4
- II Corinthians 4:17
- Daniel 12:3
- II Timothy 2:15
- Romans 10:17

    Problems then become opportunities to do something for God eternally when it is too late for the lost according to Revelation 20:14, 15, which says, *"And death and hell were cast into the lake of fire. This is the second death. And whosoever was not found written in* the book of life was cast into the lake of fire." There is not one person in Hell that would not trade places with me—even if only for a little while.

5. PASSING. Some day we will pass from this world into the arms of Jesus. It matters much how we will be remembered— "They suffered tragedy but did not quit." "His back was broken but not his spirit." But most important is how we will be received. We want to hear Jesus say, "...*Well done, good and faithful servant; thou hast been faithful over a few things, I will make thee ruler over many things: enter thou into the joy of thy lord.*" (Matthew 26:21)

Galatians 2:20, "*I am crucified with Christ: nevertheless I live; yet not I, but Christ liveth in me: and the life which I [WE] now live in the flesh I [WE] live by the faith of the Son of God, who loved me, and gave himself for me.*"

Meet More of My Friends...

Top left: Bonnie Britt
Top right: Marge Jones

Below left: Dan and Caroline Daniel
Below right: Belinda and Bob Gaona

How to Stay Up When Life Gets You Down

by Cricket Boyd

Bill and I met when we were 15 years old, and as young adults we became man and wife. When we stood before our pastor and took our vows, we didn't add any "if thens," "what ifs," or "as long as," in our lifelong commit‑ment to each other. Though we were young, we knew that mar‑riage was for life.

We were reared just the opposite of each other. Bill was reared in a Christian home where going to church was never a question. I was reared around barrooms and dance halls, where church was never mentioned.

Bill and Cricket Boyd with Roy and Joy Moffitt

At the tender age of five, Bill was led to the Lord by his father while living in Salt Lake City, Utah. Bill led me to the Lord at the age of sixteen, and that night I followed my decision with baptism.

Bill and I always knew that we had a very different relationship than most couples our age. We knew that our lives would be different, on purpose. This was the choice that we made together. This commitment to each other strengthened our relationship and gave a purpose in our lives.

In February 1999 our bond to each other would be tested to the limits. Bill was involved in a construction accident which left him a quadriplegic for life. When the accident happened, I knew that God had a plan for our lives and a purpose for what was about to come.

The road to recovery was very long and tiresome. There were days that seemed to go on forever when the pain was endless; and then there were times that we would see some small improvement on Bill's part, and our hopes of recovery would be encouraged.

Bill and I would always pray together, even though he was in a coma. Our daughter Tisha and I would sing "What a Day That Will Be" before leaving to go home for the night. The trip home would be one filled with prayer, tears, and a flood of memories of our lives together. I didn't know if Bill would still be living when I arrived the next morning, or if he would recognize me when he came out of the coma. There were times that Bill's eyes would be open, but he would look right through me as if I was not there.

With the challenges that were set before us, we chose to look for the good and for the opportunities to serve our Lord to the fullest. We knew that others were looking to us to see how to "make it." As JoJo Moffitt says, "Fake it till you make it!"

As all of us know, God will not put more on you than you can handle, and I have always said, "God must think that my shoulders are very large; so if He thinks they are, then so will I."

God has bonded our hearts with others who are hurting and having trials. He has given us the opportunity to serve in the ministry as missionaries to missionaries and pastors. One of the newest ministries that we have started is "My Sister's Keeper." This ministry consists of being there for sisters in Christ after a life-changing situations happen. We are there for them more than just the typical two weeks. We do not want to forget the ones who are hurting and go on with everyday life because forgetting about them does not heal their hurt. This ministry gives a visible meaning to all of the trials which we have endured.

Bill and Cricket Boyd renewed their wedding vows on their thirtieth anniversary at First Baptist Church of Hammond, Indiana. Roy and I served as attendants.

Meet More of My Friends...

The Tim Dotson family

Top: Tim and Jean Dotson

Center: Joy and Sam Pomeroy
and Autumn

Below: Alex and Holly Davila
and A.J.

Rebekah's Story

by Stuart Mason

Sweet Rebekah Mason

Sunday, September 2, 2001, dawned as a typical day in our home. However, it would prove to be a day that changed our lives forever. God had blessed me with a wonderful wife, Toni, and four beautiful daughters. Amanda was fourteen, Kristen was eleven, Lauren would soon be six, and Rebekah had recently celebrated her first birthday. We were living in Somerset, Kentucky, and we were serving in Ferguson, Kentucky, at the Maranatha Baptist Church where I was the pastor.

It was Labor Day weekend, and my wife's parents were spending the weekend with us. Not only are they family, but they are also two of the finest Christians I know. They have been the model grandparents, and our girls always looked forward to their visits.

After the Sunday evening service, we went to Dairy Queen for some food, fun, and fellowship. We were joined by several members of our church. After a short time, Toni and her mother took the girls home to get them ready for bed. My mother-in-law, Mrs. Fowler, always loved to help, especially with her grandchildren.

On this night, she offered to bathe the two younger girls. This was certainly the providence of God. Mrs. Fowler was a nurse for a general surgeon for many years. Upon lifting Rebekah from the tub, she felt something peculiar in her abdomen area. Mr. Fowler and I arrived at the house some time later. Toni and her mother were waiting at the door. I could see they were noticeably upset, but I had no idea what was wrong. They told me about Rebekah, and Mrs. Fowler felt that it was serious. A friend of mine was a doctor on call at our local hospital. He came to the house and thoroughly examined Rebekah. He advised us to get tests immediately.

In the hours that followed, sleep could not be found. We were heavy with the thoughts of what tomorrow might bring. However, we knew Who held tomorrow. Monday was Labor Day, and very few tests were run at our hospital. On Tuesday Rebekah had a CT scan and was given a preliminary diagnosis of hepatoblastoma. In simple terms, our beautiful 12-month old daughter had liver cancer.

We were immediately sent to Cincinnati Children's Hospital, 200 miles from our home. On Wednesday Rebekah underwent her first surgery. The surgeons planned to do a biopsy to see if the tumor was indeed cancerous, and they were hoping to remove the tumor during this surgery. Not long into the surgery, my wife and I were called into a consultation room. The doctors told us they could not remove the tumor because it was too close to the main artery going into the liver.

The following Tuesday was September 11, 2001—now known as 9-11! On that day Rebekah received her first round of chemotherapy. It is amazing how quickly your life can change. Our lives changed dramatically, and it seemed like the whole world stopped. In the midst of the difficulties in Rebekah's life, we were able to clearly see the Lord working in the lives of our family, our church, and our countless friends.

Rebekah would ultimately receive several rounds of three different kinds of chemotherapy. She had five surgeries, including one that involved removing the cancerous tumor and a large portion of her liver. She received several blood transfusions, spent countless nights in the hospital, and lost all of her blonde hair. Rebekah had little chance of survival, yet God was faithful and merciful. We thank Him for His guiding hand, for the many doctors and nurses who touched our lives and who were so good to Rebekah, and for His enduring grace and mercy. We praise Him for His many mighty works on behalf of Rebekah and our family. During the many long nights, we would feel God's presence. We are thankful for the many prayers that were offered—some by people we do not even know.

In April 2007 Rebekah was given a clean bill of health and moved to "survivor" status. We praise God for all He has done and for all that He continues to do. What a mighty God we serve!

The Stuart Mason family

Meet More of My Friends...

Above (left to right):
Matt, Jamie, and Eddie Lapina

Below (left to right):
Tevor, Troy, Brian, Trinity, and Jamie Hasse

My Father's Joy

by Bill Burr, Jr.

I would like to begin by explaining how I was asked to author this chapter. My father is the subject of this chapter and was originally asked to pen it. However, because of medical reasons, he has been unable to do so. My father just came home from the hospital two days ago. He underwent surgery to open a blockage in his bile duct. Just 19 days prior, he had undergone a very similar surgery to open a blockage in his duodenum. Because of the deadlines for publishing this book, it was not possible that he would be able to pen this chapter.

Our buddy,
Bill Burr
———

Therefore, the author has asked me to step in and write it in his stead. Keep this in mind as you read the remainder of the chapter, realizing that my words could not relate the story as my father's could. My prayer, though, is that it will be a blessing and perhaps an inspiration for those of us looking to have a little more joy in our lives.

Both of the surgeries I mentioned are the results of only side effects of a much larger medical problem. The root of the problem is a cancerous tumor that lies on top of Dad's pancreas and next to his stomach and duodenal passage. The tumor has grown in size and has caused the above-mentioned blockages. He (and my

Bill and Patsy Burr

mom, Patsy) have been battling this problem since its discovery a couple of years ago. Several battles have occurred over the past two years. The first battle was an attempt to operate and remove the tumor surgically. We lost that battle. The second battle was to utilize chemotherapy in order to stop the cancerous tumor. Although the cancer did go into remission for about five months, it returned. Subsequently, Dad has undergone three additional rounds of chemotherapy. I believe that the chemotherapy did add some extension to life, but because of the reduced medical benefits and increased side effects, these treatments were stopped.

The third battle was an attempt to use a specialized radiation treatment called the "CyberKnife" to kill the cancerous tumor. Two separate treatments with the "CyberKnife" were performed. Again, I believe some extension of life was gained, but the cancer has remained. He is now undergoing a treatment with a medication called Vectibix, realizing that this drug only has positive effects in 30 percent of its patients.

Let me also relate some other medical battles that have been going on during recent years. Dad has also undergone open-heart bypass surgery. He has had about eight stints to open heart blockages. He has had radioactive seed implants to battle prostate cancer. He battles kidney stones. He has had his gallbladder removed. He suffers from Paget's Disease, which causes a reduction of strength in his bones. He has had several inches of his colon surgically removed in order to remove another tumor. And the list continues....

Now you are thinking, "Why was anyone like this asked to

write a chapter on JOY?" The answer is because through it all, **JOY REMAINETH!**

At this time in my own life, I have realized what some may call the "cycle of life." Allow me to explain:

1. A child is born and cannot take care of himself. The child knows when something is wrong but does not have the ability to do anything about it.
2. The child matures to the point that he can be instructed how to manage his own needs. He cannot operate on his own, but with the aid of a parent, care can be accomplished.
3. The child grows into an adult and is able to care solely for his own needs.
4. The adult grows older and realizes that he can still take care of his own personal needs but requires the assistance of someone else.
5. The adult grows old to the point where he cannot take care of himself. He knows when something is wrong but does not have the ability within to do anything about it.

We are all somewhere in this cycle. We may not want to admit where we are, but we are in the cycle. I feel that I am currently in Step 3. I feel that my dad is somewhere between Step 4 and Step 5. I am sure that he will let me know where he stands when he reads this.

Salvation can come at any point on the cycle mentioned above. Some will receive salvation during Step 1 of the cycle, and some will receive salvation during Step 5 of the cycle. It is key to realize that no matter where salvation enters the cycle, it REMAINS throughout. Because true joy is a fruit of the Spirit (Galatians 3:22) and can only be realized after salvation, we can conclude that joy can enter the cycle only after salvation has, and it, too, should REMAIN throughout the remainder of the cycle.

My dad was saved when he was 24 years old—Step 3 on the cycle of life. I believe Isaiah 61:10 describes something his soul got right after it was washed in the blood of Christ. *"I will greatly rejoice in the LORD, my soul shall be joyful in my God; for he hath clothed me with the garments of salvation, he hath covered me with the robe of righteousness, as a bridegroom decketh himself with ornaments, and as a bride adorneth herself with her jewels."* This joy is something that my dad has never lost.

Another characteristic of my dad is his boldness. Some of my earliest childhood memories with Dad are going to the radio station every week. Dad had a weekly preaching broadcast. Every week I can remember his beginning the broadcast with Romans 1:16, *"For I am not ashamed of the gospel of Christ: for it is the power of God unto salvation to every one that believeth; to the Jew first, and also to the Greek."* He has never been ashamed of his salvation or his joy since he received Christ as his everlasting Saviour when he was 24 years old.

I believe that the combination of these two Biblical characteristics of my dad is the reason why he was asked to participate in this book. He has boldness about his joy. Even as I write these words, I am being convicted by the Holy Spirit because I (we), too, should have these Biblical qualities so clearly in my life as presented in Isaiah and Romans.

A few years after Dad was saved, he took his salvation, joy, and boldness, along with a call to preach, to Bible college. In 1965 at age 30, he enrolled in Tennessee Temple. While at Tennessee Temple, he enhanced his joy and boldness with Jeremiah 15:16, which says, *"Thy words were found, and I did eat them; and thy word was unto me the joy and rejoicing of mine heart: for I am called by thy name, O LORD God of hosts."* Dad graduated from Bible college in 1968 (the year I was born) and left to serve the Lord with a salvation, a joy, a boldness, a calling, and the Word of God under his arm.

Since that time, so many have grown to know and love my dad. I believe that most are drawn to Dad because of the qualities I have mentioned. Dad has always preached, sung, lived, and testified in this light. Many people, including myself, may have one or some of these qualities, but rarely do we find someone with all of them simultaneously. This combination is not natural; it is Biblical and available to all.

Now we come to the subject matter of this book—*even more joy*. How is it possible to live such a joyful life for the Lord, go through so many physical trials, and have even more joy toward the end of your life? Perhaps this is the kind of joy that we find in I Peter 1:8, "*Whom having not seen, ye love; in whom, though now ye see him not, yet believing, ye rejoice with joy unspeakable and full of glory.*"

Dad realized at age 24 when he was saved, and even now, that it is all about Jesus Christ. As Dad lives in the senior years of life, he does not have the physical abilities to display his internal joy as he once did. I can remember when Dad would sing several specials, preach a 45-minute sermon, sing a few more specials, then stay and talk to people after services. I can remember how he would shout and run the aisle of the church when his heart would overflow with joy about his salvation.

Is the joy gone because the physical displays have gone? NO! After reading I Peter 1:8 again, I have seen even more joy in my dad. I have found that words not spoken can be read by the eyes. This joy is displayed even more when I drop by his house and find him weeping over the words of the Bible—more joy as he struggles to enter the church-house doors, more joy as he witnesses to people at doctor and hospital visits, and even more joy as he continues to center his life around the One he has not seen and loves so much, Jesus Christ.

Now let's return to our discussion on the "cycle of life." What profit is there if a person enters and leaves the "cycle of life" without have affected anyone for the cause of Christ? My father has tried to affect as many lives as possible through his preaching and singing over the past 47 years. But I am starting to realize how one can obtain even more joy than this.

Judges 2:10 says, "*...and there arose another generation after them, which knew not the LORD....*" In comparison, Psalm 145:4 says, "*One generation shall praise thy works to another, and shall declare thy mighty acts.*" I do not know if Dad realized this during his life, but I do believe that he realizes it now.

One additional by-product of his life is that he has successfully passed down his Lord from his generation to his four children—Donna; Carol; Bill, Jr.; and Mary Beth. I believe that this is even more joy. As of this writing, I am enrolled in Bible college and plan to serve our Lord full time. I, too, am a father and realize what joy it would be to pass along my beliefs and my Lord to my children and grandchildren.

In summary, I believe my dad's life has given us a recipe for joy unspeakable. Take the joy of salvation shown in Isaiah 61:10. Add more joy with the boldness of Romans 1:16. Add even more joy with the Word of God as seen in Jeremiah 15:16. Center your life around the Lord Jesus Christ and live to affect as many people in the "cycle of life" for the cause of Christ.

The Yo-Yo
by Renee Cox

What a joy to be included in your book, JoJo. I remember the first time I saw you at Spectacular in 1976! Your laughter and enthusiasm attracted me to you from the first moment. Now for these last 30-plus years, I can still say that. Thanks for your encouragement and enthusiasm for the Lord.

My husband and I have been in the ministry for almost 39 years. The first five years were spent at a wonderful little mountain church in the hills of East Tennessee. What a joy and challenge to work with these wonderful people. Probably our most difficult challenge there was convincing the people we needed more space. Their beautiful building, built of river rock from the Nolichucky River, was just too small. My patient husband finally persuaded them to build a beautiful new auditorium, more than doubling our space. That was an exciting day when we moved into our new auditorium, complete with an indoor baptistery! We saw many people saved and baptized in our five years there.

Pastor and Mrs. Jack Cox
Son Joshua and daughter-in-law Sarah

We then moved to my home church to pastor for 10 years. Those were wonderful, but challenging days as well. Probably the biggest challenge for my husband was pastoring all his in-laws!! We learned many things during those days that brought us closer to the Lord. My husband first worked with the Christian school ministry there.

In January of 1983, the Lord led us to Liberty Baptist Church in Durham, North Carolina. Honestly, I didn't want to come. We had a new baby just five months old, a new house that we had built, and my family all around. But God had a different plan. The Sunday my husband came to preach at Liberty, I cried the whole service. (I am still teased about it!) Deep in our hearts, we knew this was God's plan for us, so we moved to Durham and began the most wonderful years of our lives!

Liberty Baptist Church was at a low point in her history— attendance was low; the school was in a state of confusion, and the people were quite discouraged. God began to work and bless. We have seen some wonderful things happen in our great city. Eleven years ago we moved from our old property to our brand-new facilities on Guess Road. However, we had no auditorium yet, just a gym. We spent seven wonderful years in that gym and watched the Lord do many wonderful works. Finally, three years ago we moved into our beautiful new auditorium.

The year of 2001 was probably one of our most difficult. My mother-in-law went to Heaven in January. Of course, Dr. Hyles went to Heaven in February, followed by my wonderful friend, Marlene Evans, in July. In October 2001, my dear friend, Mary Christ, wife of our music director, died after a long battle with bone cancer, and Kerry Peoples, our 34-year-old teacher/coach at our Christian school died of cancer, leaving behind a beautiful wife and two precious little girls. Wow, what a year! I know the Lord brought us through this hard year to prepare us to serve Him more fully in the future. I'm so glad He picks us up when we are low. I'm glad He has promised He would never leave us, or forsake us.

Someone asked me this week, "What is the most difficult thing about serving the Lord for almost 25 years at the same church?" I think I would have to say the most difficult "down" of the ministry is watching people you care for and love and for whom you have given your life, turn their back and walk away from the Lord, the church, and God's plan for their lives.

The Kerry Peoples family

In all these years in the ministry, I think I have discovered that life is like a yo-yo. I have never mastered the yo-yo thing. You see, for it to be working correctly, it must go up and down. Me, I can only get it to go down. In reality, it is beautiful when it goes up and down! My life has been a series of ups and downs, and I'm sure that's the way the Lord intended for it to be at its best. The down times are not fun, but they are very much a part of the Christian life.

Meet More of My Friends...

Above (left to right):
Linda & John Vaprezsan, Roy & JoJo Moffitt, Marge & Bill Hasse
Seated: Joy Moffitt & Todd Vaprezsan

Below: Joy Moffitt, Todd Vaprezsan, Brother and Mrs. Schaap

Joy Through Grief
by Linda Vaprezsan

"...for I will turn their mourning into joy, and will comfort them, and make them rejoice from their sorrow." (Jeremiah 31:13)

Having *joy through grief* is not a subject for which I had wanted to be known, but God has placed me here for a purpose. When you think of grief, you think of sorrow. Grief is sorrowful, but *joy* can come from that sorrow. There is no joy in death and separation, but fixing our minds and hearts beyond the moment will see us through a funeral—claiming God's promises—knowing that as believers, we will be in Heaven forever. There is no joy for the non-believer. There is no anticipation for a hereafter or a life in Heaven for eternity!

John and Linda Vaprezsan with Roy and JoJo Moffitt

Life is a series of day-by-day circumstances. Only when we fix our eyes on the Lord and His promises can we have victory and rise above the cares of this life. That eternal thread of hope—that invisible line of filament that can hold through great weight—will sustain us in difficult times. Just like a fisherman's line, God's Word is our lifeline! God's Word is our foundational Rock! God's Word is the anchor that holds us steady when the chaos of life around us is in a tumult!

Yes, we have good days and awful days—sad days and jubilant days, but to experience the calming sustaining inner joy, we must turn to the Lord daily and keep our inner batteries charged with His Word. Most people never let their cell phone go dead; once they do, their ability to communicate becomes nil. We keep our cell phones plugged into the source of power! So it is with our hearts and minds. We must stay in touch where the power is—through prayer and God's Word.

God allowed us a little time to prepare for the deaths of a few of our people. Preparing for their deaths brought us closer as a church and as a family. We fasted, prayed, grocery shopped, made meals, etc. This helped our people feel a part of what was going on.

———

From May 2006 through May 2007, our church went through one of the toughest times through which a church can go. Our church is like a close family, and when one hurts another hurts. We have gone through several hurts this past year.

In May 2006 we lost one of our dearest ladies, age 37, to cancer. She left a husband and three children. Her death was very difficult on all. We had prayed for a miracle, but God knew better and relieved her of her pain and suffering. She and her husband worked with our church teenagers. Not only was Becky a blessing to Preacher and myself, but she was my daughter-in-law's best friend. Her husband was our youngest son's Sunday school teacher and now our grandson's Sunday school teacher.

Three months after the passing of Becky, we were faced with the death of another one of our dear ladies to cancer. Ashley died at the age of 38, leaving a husband and four children. She and her husband worked with our bus teenagers and were such a blessing to them. Ashley was our daughter's best friend. So within three months my daughter and daughter-in-law lost their best friends.

Pictured left: Ashley Johnson and her family
Pictured right: Becky Prater and her family

Then in the fall, one of our men, 46 years old, a former bus captain, deacon, and Sunday school teacher, died suddenly. This loss of course was a shock to us and to his dear family. He left a wife and seven children. His death affected our son John who is our bus director. His wife is a dear friend of mine. They were both very involved in the church.

Then in May 2007, God took one of dear Christian school teachers. Yvonne was 45 years old and had two blood diseases which caused her to have congestive heart failure. We did not know she was that sick until two months before her passing,

Yvonne with Todd
———

although we thought she would pull through until the day before she died. She was single but left a church family who grieved for her deeply.

Yvonne taught our son Todd and our granddaughter Alexis in kindergarten and taught PE to our daughter Pamela. She had been a member of our church since she was 14 and taught in our Christian school for 22 years. On the night of her kindergarten class graduation, Yvonne also graduated to Heaven, just 20 minutes after being told of her class graduating.

The people who died not only left behind their spouses, but 13 unmarried children. It was now our job to be an encouragement to these children. We had to convey hope to all left behind. We had to show them *joy*.

Our bodies and minds must have time to heal. We are made to feel the emotions of pain and suffering. If we never suffer, how would we know or learn to appreciate joy and happiness? If we never experienced rain, how would we know to appreciate sunshine? If we never had a problem, how could we appreciate the grace of God to see us through the difficult situations in life? It is a cycle that God has created that we might appreciate His qualities and His greatness.

Life must go on. The day after Ashley died, my daughter had already planned a birthday party for Ashley's daughter Layne and her own daughter Micaela. Their birthdays are on the same day. Even though Ashley had died the day before, they went ahead with the party. She wanted to make this party a joyous time! Even through the sorrow, they were able to find joy.

The children of our church had to learn grief at a young age, but God brings *joy* out of mourning. We have a very loving church family who rallied around these families. We wanted to be a blessing to them.

The ladies of our church tried to make this sorrowful time a joyful time for Becky and Ashley. They planned a head-shaving party for Becky. Becky craved Whopper Jr.'s during the last few weeks, so we would do Whopper runs for her. It was also a joke among our ladies that Becky always had a supply of chocolate when anyone had a chocolate craving.

Two years before Ashley died, she went through an extensive double mastectomy and reconstruction surgery with the hopes of warding off a recurrence of her cancer. The ladies had a farewell to the old Ashley "look," complete with games, jokes, gifts, testimonies, etc. These times helped us all deal with the cancer with *more joy* than sitting around feeling sorry for everyone involved.

After their deaths everyone started asking "Why?" but, "Why not us?" Are we better than Job? God has a purpose for each of our lives. There is a time to be born and a time to die. We may think this is too early to die, but this was all in God's plan.

It became our job to be an encourager. We had to paste on a smile for everyone to see. This is not easy when your heart is breaking, but this is what our people needed to see. Much of our lack of joy is ignorance of God's Word. We worry when we should trust. The more saturated we are in His Word, the more we can trust what is going on around us. Even *in the midst* of heartache, pain, and difficult circumstances, He is there, working out His will.

There is no joy in sadness, heartache, loss, tragedy, or pain, but we can rise above the moment by relying on God's Word. God's Word gives hope, encouragement, strength to endure, strength for the journey, peace in the midst of chaos; He alone is able to bring us out of the fiery test and situation. When we look to the Lord and rely on His promises, our joy will return in time. Our inner sense of happiness will return because we trust in Him. He is our joy!

These deaths have taught all of us to appreciate the life God has given us. Psalm 30:5 says, *"....weeping may endure for a night, but joy cometh in the morning."* Life is too short for us to not have **even more joy** through the ups and downs of life.

The Vaprezsan clan

The Wreck
by Loretta Walker

My family has traveled in evangelism for nearly 20 years. We are in a different church nearly every week, traveling about 25,000 miles a year. We traveled in a medium-duty Freightliner truck and fifth wheel trailer until we had an accident with a near fatality on May 14, 2004. The truck separated from the trailer and rolled twice, and the trailer rolled once leaving pieces as it rolled. Both were literally in pieces at the end of the crash.

Miraculously, my husband was the only one of the five of us who was injured. Tears fill my eyes as I write this with gratitude for God's saving our lives. I remember when I was riding in the trailer and realized that we were going to wreck. I told God, "I trust You with this."

Kevin and Loretta
Walker
with Jeannie Mae,
K.W., and Joe

When you look at the pictures, you would wonder—as all of us do—how anyone could walk away from such a crash. The only thing I can say is that God sent holy angels to protect us and keep us safe.

After the initial accident, I had several extremely hard times. The first came when I was standing by my injured husband who was lying on the road, bloody and in horrendous pain. I would look at him, then look at my three frightened children, and then at our little Jack Russell terrier. I knew the ambulance was on the way, but I didn't know whether I should stay with the wreckage and the children or go with Kevin to the hospital. When the ambulance finally arrived, I watched the emergency personnel load Kevin and close the door. I'll never forget how it felt to watch the ambulance pull away, knowing it was quite possible that I wouldn't see him again. Of course, at that time I didn't know the extent of his injuries.

After the ambulance left, I was faced with the dilemma of being in the middle of a highway with many people around but not really any one person to help me. I asked firemen, police officers, and others who was in charge and who would help me know what to do next. No one could tell me. I had moved my kids from the truck, to some kind Samaritan's car, and finally to the backseat of the fire truck. K.W. stayed by my side helping me try to retrieve shoes, jackets, anything that might help me through the next few hours. At that point, all I cared about were the next few hours. One fireman found a credit card lying in the grass and a one dollar bill. We only found one shoe for my youngest son; the rest of us were hardly dressed for public viewing. Finally a salvage man arrived, and the police officer called for another car to come and take the four of us to the hospital.

I huddled in the back seat with K.W., Joe, and the dog, while Jeannie rode in the front seat. On the 30-minute trip to the next town, I asked the officer, "What should we do about our dog?"

He chuckled and said, "I don't know."

I asked if he knew of a nearby motel which would allow us to keep a pet. We had to stop at a couple before we found one that would allow us to have Jack. As I escorted our bedraggled group to the room, people were obviously watching us. I don't blame the people for staring at us as they were getting their breakfast in the lobby. If we could have traded places, I know I would have stared in curiosity at our crew!

The second hardest time for me came when I had to shut that motel door and leave my children alone in that room. I did it quickly with as much assurance as I could muster, giving assurance of a call as soon as I knew anything. Outside in the hall I paused to pray to thank God that we had taught the children how to have a relationship with their Heavenly Father. I asked Him to be especially close to them.

When the policeman and I arrived at the hospital, we had some difficulty finding Kevin. He had been taken to the surgical ICU, which was unusual. When I finally arrived at the waiting room, the nurses were changing shifts. So I sat there with no information for seemingly like an eternity. The waiting room was full of sleeping individuals who were waiting on loved ones inside that ICU. I looked at my mud-covered shoes and legs and evaluated my wool coat, my mud-splashed skirt, my wrinkled shirt, my flat hair, and no makeup. I decided I must look like a bag lady to that room full of people. I sat for a brief moment and decided I'd better call someone to help me keep from falling apart. I called a friend whom I thought wouldn't mind an early morning call. When she answered, I calmly told her of the accident and told her I needed someone to help me stay calm until the nurse would give me some kind of report. We talked for a few minutes; she helped me keep my sanity, and then I hung up to wait for someone to come out of ICU with some news. I didn't have many numbers memorized, and my cell phone was not one of the items I found as I pilfered through the wreckage in the dark, so I didn't call anyone else.

As I sat there physically alone, I reminded myself of the song that had come to mind while I was standing in the middle of the road. I only knew a few of the words of the chorus, but I had used it as a prayer: "He's in the midst of my storm; He's in the valley we walk through; where two or three are gathered in His name, He'll be there, too!" God and I had a neat little talk. He hugged me over and over and tried to convince me that everything was going to be all right.

During those hours in the hospital in a room full of hurting people, I sat engulfed in the watchcare and protection of the Heavenly Father. That time was beautiful. I didn't cry much then because I believe I was in shock from the trauma of the whole situation. I sang that phrase of the song over and over, letting my heart know that God was with me. I kept telling God that I could make it as long as He would be with me.

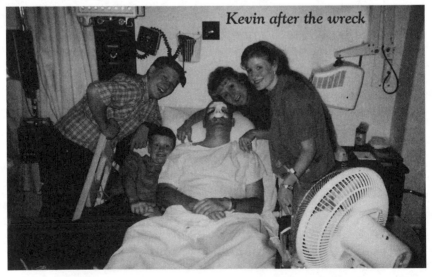

Kevin after the wreck

The Wreck

Remember the dollar the fireman found in the wreckage? I went to the Coke machine and bought a Diet Coke! It comforted me, too. God had given me that one dollar so I could have that bit of enjoyment during a trying time.

God was very real to me during those few hours right after the wreck. He was right beside me when I heard the doctor's reports. He helped me during my first call to our insurance company, and the secretary told me our policy couldn't be found. He helped me by sending a preacher in the area to get clothes for the children and bring them to me at the hospital. He helped me by giving me literally hundreds of phone calls from all over the nation to encourage me and to help me know that people were praying for us.

I could never have made it through this traumatic time without God. Jeremiah 29:11 says, *"For I know the thoughts that I think toward you, saith the LORD, thoughts of peace, and not of evil, to give you an expected end."* A friend emailed me this verse, and it became my thought with each waking minute. I trusted God through this situation, knowing He had something in mind for my family.

You too would be wise to develop a close relationship to the Word of God and to your Heavenly Father in order to prepare yourself for possible devastation. I adopted a song and a verse to help my troubled mind get through that hard time. I'll be honest—the first few days after the wreck, I could not focus long enough to get much out of the Bible. I tried reading a Gideon Bible while in the waiting room. I looked at words that I couldn't understand. God gave me that verse and brought to my mind many other verses that I had memorized that helped me. I trust these thoughts have encouraged you on how to go through a tragedy.

- Get a song.
- Get a verse.

- Realize that your Heavenly Father is close to you and wants to help you.
- Keep a journal of how you see God work. One of the first things I had written in my journal when I got some paper was that God gave me a dollar so I could purchase that Diet Coke in the waiting room!

Our smashed truck

Our 40-foot fifth-wheel trailer in pieces at the scene of the accident

My Battle With Cancer
by Katherine Schulz

When I was asked to share my story regarding my cancer, I felt that mine was not that great of a story. I was fighting the disease as I thought everyone would do in my situation. Then the Lord reminded me of Philippians 1:6 that says when He works in your life, it is a great work. *"Being confident of this very thing, that he which hath begun a good work in you will perform it until the day of Jesus Christ."* I can be confident that God is working in my life using the cancer. He will continue to work in my life until I meet Him in Heaven.

Mrs. Evans coined the phrase, "Cancer, my friend." Yes, you can be confident that God will not bring something into your life that would hurt you. This phrase may have made my first response concerning cancer a positive one.

The Calvin Schulz family

In Luke 11:13, the Bible says, *"If ye then, being evil, know how to give good gifts unto your children: how much more shall your heavenly Father give the Holy Spirit to them that ask Him?"* God made me, He saved me, and He will not give His children evil gifts. If God has begun a good work in me, I can believe that cancer is a good gift from my Heavenly Father. I told my family the first week of my diagnosis of cancer, "If anyone should have cancer in my family, I would rather it be me."

Another statement Mrs. Evans made was, "Cancer? Why not?" instead of asking "Why cancer?" Should we question God working in our life? No! The Bible says in James 1:17, *"Every good gift and every perfect gift is from above, and cometh down from the Father of lights, with whom is no variableness, neither shadow of turning."*

When you know that you are a child of God and your life is in His hands, why would death be anything to fear? You will have a new body and will be in the presence of Jesus. But for those who do not know Christ Jesus as their Saviour, there would be great fear. When an unsaved person leaves this world without knowing Christ, that person leaves behind all the good he will ever know and enter into an eternity without God.

God began working in my life as a five-year-old girl. I learned that Jesus loved me from Mrs. Shirley Moore, my Sunday school teacher. At age ten, I went to stay a week with my cousin Carolyn Sue. There my Aunt Audrey taught me that my heart was black with sin and the blood of Jesus could wash it white as snow. But it was not until the fall of 1973 that I was 100 percent sure that I would go to Heaven. My cousin Karl shared what the Bible said regarding salvation. It all came together that day. That is when I knew how to go to Heaven and accepted God's gift of eternal life.

I began attending regularly an independent Baptist church. I began reading my Bible. One thing began to happen—the Word of God began to dwell in my heart richly. The Holy Spirit was teaching me, and my faith began to grow. I fell in love with its words and began memorizing it so I could witness to my friends. Later I began learning complete chapters and books for our champion Bible quiz team. As a teenager I enjoyed winning a trophy on our church's quiz team. Learning God's Word would prepare me to stand before God someday.

I met my husband Calvin during my fourth year of Bible college. It was a smart choice. We have weathered many of the storms in our lives together. His faith has made it possible to believe God would use cancer to strengthen our family.

We all would like to live a long and prosperous life in the Lord. But God has a set time for each of us to die. We must live our lives in a way that we look unto the Lord to come and take us away every day. We should be faithful in every way.

When I was a child, I desired to learn music. I joined the school band in the sixth grade. Before entering high school, I was asked to learn to play the oboe. I enjoyed playing the oboe for the four years of school but did not play another oboe until I was in my forties. Following the direction and wisdom of Dr. Schaap, the First Baptist Church started an orchestra. I thought it would be nice to play again, but I was already faithful to the church choir.

One night after choir practice the Lord convicted me to join the orchestra to play my oboe. A few weeks later the orchestra director, Brother Clyde Wolfe, asked me to join. I believed God was moving me. I never realized that my obligation to the orchestra would help me desire to get well. I never liked letting people down—especially when they needed me.

In the fall of 2006, we had a great trip to Colorado, where we spent time with Calvin's family. We went to visit my family during Thanksgiving and enjoyed seeing everyone. During Christmas things could not have been better. By the time the New Year rolled in, my body started changing. My physical change was not from an improper diet; our family had begun eating organic food.

In January 2006, while working on staff at Hyles-Anderson College, my physical change became more noticeable. My first thoughts were that my pancreatic problems had returned. After blood tests were taken, I learned it was not the pancreas. Later a CAT scan revealed that I had ovarian cancer.

When my doctor realized that my condition was severe, he seemed to panic and wanted me to rush to the hospital for tests and into emergency surgery. I was not alarmed at the news. It was time for my daughter Hannah to be picked up from school. She was in her senior year, and it bothered the doctor that I was more concerned about picking her up than my serious condition. I explained that God made me and knew all about my condition. I assured him that I was not afraid to die and that I knew Christ as my Saviour and was going to Heaven when I died. I explained what the Bible said about our appointment to die. If it was my time to die, I would not be late for the appointment.

Ovarian cancer is called "the silent killer." I did not feel any pain. I continued to work until I felt that I needed some concrete evidence of my condition. When my husband Calvin and I met with Dr. Dennis Streeter, we set up surgery for the following Saturday. Surgery was necessary. We were told the following options:

- No surgery—weeks to live
- Surgery, no chemo—months to live
- Surgery and chemo—year or two to live
- Surgery and chemo with a change in lifestyle—two to five years if we did all that we knew to do and trusted the Lord—who knew what God had in store for my life.

After meeting with Dr. Streeter, my husband Calvin and I knew my life was in God's hands.

We arranged a meeting with our pastor at the college where

he would pray with us and anoint me with oil. At that meeting Dr. Schaap explained that I would win either way: if my surgery went successfully, I could begin the fight against cancer and have extended time with my family and church. If it was God's will to take me to Heaven, I would win because I would be with Jesus in a cancer-free body.

Dr. Schaap wanted me to study my illness and become an expert. He explained that 95 percent of people with a cancer diagnosis die because they give up. I needed to believe I was of the 5 percent who was going to fight. He wanted me to be in the center of all my decisions regarding my cancer and not let the doctors control me. I later found out that most cancer patients never ask questions nor know what the doctors are doing. I would often give my pastor's advice to other cancer patients when they asked why I was so knowledgeable about my treatments.

Because of this wisdom, no one should go through an illness or a cancer fight without first consulting with the pastor. Doctors cannot comfort you the way your pastor can. The Scriptures encourage your heart. When you hear your pastor's prayers, you realize that God is already working toward answering his prayers. When you hear him praying and asking God to extend your life, you will receive great peace.

I asked my brother Mike and my sister Laura to be present when I went in for prayer and an anointing with oil. I was asking everyone to pray that I would be able to play my oboe in the orchestra during Pastors' School.

I even asked Dr. Schaap to pray for one special request: "Could you pray that I could play my oboe in the church orchestra for Pastors' School?" The oboe has an unusual sound, and the selected music had important oboe solos. My prayer was not to ruin the special music for Pastors' School. I didn't want to bring the burden on anyone to learn the instrument. After several minutes of encouragement and faith building, we were all trusting God that I could make it to Pastors' School.

I remember telling my family: "If anyone was going to have cancer, I was glad it was me." That statement may have sounded strange to them, but I knew I didn't want any one else to suffer. Suffering with God's grace is not really suffering.

On Saturday, March 11, 2006, I underwent cancer surgery. Dr. Colsten met with my family for prayer before surgery. My mother, brother, sister, and many members of their families were there to meet with me. We had to move to a larger room to accommodate the size of the crowd.

Then one other man walked in, bowed his head in prayer, and asked God to begin to work and to assist in the surgery. When he left, one of my brothers-in-law asked if that was another preacher from my church. I said, "No, that was my surgeon, Dr. Dennis Streeter." When your surgeon prays for you before he begins his work, you can believe God will be working as the Great Physician.

After the two-hour surgery, I remained in the hospital for two days. I began to care for myself. I knew the only way to get on my feet again was actually to get up on my feet.

I had several visitors from church and work who encouraged me. I would ask them to pray that I could attend Pastors' School.

When I was dismissed from the hospital, I realized it was going to take some time to get into shape. By Thursday afternoon, I decided to put my oboe together and try to play. At that moment, Mrs. Wolfe, our orchestra director's wife and daughter Nicole dropped by to visit. They walked in on my attempt to play the music. (At least they knew I was trying!)

On the following Sunday, the day before Pastors' School, I went to church wanting to see if I could handle the crowd and play in the orchestra. If I could not handle the pressure of playing for our home crowd, I would not be able to play for those visiting from across America and the world. Little did I know that James Belisle, who loves the challenge of learning a new instrument, had begun to practice the oboe. He began practicing when he heard the news of my cancer. With his support, I made it through the services.

After the Sunday service, I felt more confident that the Lord would give me grace and strength to do my part. It was incredible how God can give you strength when you will depend on Him. What encouragement I received from everyone. They said they had been praying for me, and it was evident their prayers were answered.

It was a great week. I played each night and sat through each of the services. Many came to see me before each evening. I was totally blessed because God did want to use me.

Two weeks after surgery, I met with the oncologist to discuss my chemo treatment. My husband Calvin did not like the idea of all those chemicals flooding my system and began building my immune system with natural supplements. He wanted to fortify my body against those dangerous drugs. In addition, I met with Dr. Cal Streeter who laid out my defense for chemo. He gave me a pep talk. He wanted me to take charge of the situation and be a fighter. His encouragement kept me asking questions and seeking ways to keep on top of things.

When I began my very first chemo treatment, I told the Lord that I wanted to read through my Bible during each chemo treatment. By the end of the year, I had eight chemo treatments and completed the Bible eight times.

While going through my Bible, I found many verses that applied to my need. The first major verse was in John 15:3, which says, *"Now ye are clean through the word which I have spoken unto you."* I wanted God's Word to cleanse my heart and to renew my mind. Shortly after I claimed this verse, Dr. Schaap used this verse in one of his sermons on prayer. I felt as if God was confirming that He was going to give me the grace and strength to combat the chemo.

Proverbs 3:8 says, *"It* [God's Law] *shall be health to thy navel, and marrow to thy bones."* My stomach needed the most healing, and the marrow is where the blood is made. I wanted to be strong and healthy while going through my chemo treatments. From the time I was diagnosed with cancer, I was able to attend church on nearly every Sunday morning and evening.

Another Bible verse that I used several times when testifying of God's work in my life is from II Peter 3:14, *"Wherefore, beloved, seeing that ye look for such things, be diligent that ye may be found of him in peace, without spot, and blameless."* The portion of the verse, *"without spot,"* was the section I would pray. I would tell the new nurses my testimony and that I was praying for the spots to be removed. But when I look back, I believe He also gave me peace.

Many times I was able to witness to others how I was combating the chemo. On several occasions I witnessed to the nurses about how I claimed the promises from the Bible. I explained that God made me, He knew I had cancer, and He was the One to know how to heal me. It may have amused some, but I kept my Bible by my side during all the chemo sessions.

I wanted my family to go about their normal business. We saw our daughter Hannah graduate from Hammond Baptist High School. We did not miss her induction to the National Honor Society; we hosted her graduation party.

Our daughter Elizabeth finished her second year at Hyles-Anderson College. I hated that I wasn't there for her. I noticed that her teachers encouraged her often. She wrote a special poem for me on Mother's Day.

Our daughter Rachel was a great help to me. She would take me to my chemo sessions when her father or my sister Laura could not drive me. The sessions lasted for six hours, and I am grateful for their time with me.

My sister Gladys came for one of my last chemo sessions and saw all the details about my cancer. In November her son Tommy was diagnosed with leukemia. I never dreamed that we would have two family members fighting cancer at the same time. We spent many days encouraging each other.

I believe my success during chemo was due to the support I received from my family and friends at church. I received cards daily from people who were praying for me, some of whom were going through severe health problems.

One example was Mrs. JoJo Moffitt. She would call me often to say she had been praying for me. She met with me one afternoon for lunch and encouraged me with her love and belief that I would pull through the different stages through which I was going. She mentioned that she would not take a bite without praying for me. We all need a friend who will pray for us—especially when we are not certain of the future.

After several months of treatments, I had the normal range for cancer count. When I neared the end of my chemo sessions, I met with Dr. Schaap. I wanted life to be just as it was before cancer, but it was never going to be the same. I had thought everything would get back to normal, if I could only get through the chemo cycles. I spoke to Dr. Schaap about working again.

I believed I could handle the same load as before cancer. Under his advice I planned to train others on the oboe for the upcoming college semester. In January when the new semester began, I told everyone that I was going to teach private lessons by faith. I didn't know what was ahead with my cancer fight. I received word from the oncologist that my count was rising.

When I went to see Dr. Schaap, he suggested that I go to the Mayo Clinic. While I was waiting for the appointment with Mayo,

Dr. Streeter suggested that I begin my chemo right away. The blood test showed that even with the chemo treatment, my CA-125 tumor marker was still rising. Apparently my cancer had returned with a vengeance.

While waiting on my appointment with the Mayo Clinic, I received a note from Mrs. Cindy Schaap. She wanted me to know that she was praying for me and that I was going to get through this. Not knowing what was ahead, I took increased comfort that she was praying for me.

The Mayo Clinic called and said they could schedule me in February. I looked at the calendar and chose a later date because I was scheduled to teach in Sunday school on February 18. It was also the first day my daughter Rachel was to take her position as teacher in the Beginner II Department. My appointment was scheduled for the following Monday.

When that Sunday arrived, I knew the Lord was with me as I taught the Bible lesson. I talked to Mrs. Erma McKinney before the class. I explained that I did not want to miss teaching. I did not know when or if I would teach again.

That Sunday afternoon, my family felt a real concern for me because I had not eaten a real meal nor passed any food for several weeks. My son Jacob asked if I was going to be all right. I told him that I was going to be fine. I assured him that I would be here for quite a long time. I was mostly relieved that I was going to get a second opinion from the experts at the Mayo Clinic.

The tests taken by the doctors at the Mayo Clinic revealed that the cancer had wrapped its way around my large intestine, causing my digestive system to stop. The oncologists recommended a procedure to expand my intestine and then wait for my system to work normally before surgery for cancer.

The first attempt was unsuccessful, so a repeat was scheduled. While undergoing this second procedure, my colon tore. I was rushed into emergency surgery. It was life-threatening; my body went into septic shock.

During the surgery, Calvin called the family to ask for prayer. My children, daughter-in-law, granddaughter, and my sister Laura drove to the clinic. They arrived after my seven and one-half hours of surgery. Dr. Bobbi Gostout, the surgeon, said she would have worked longer at removing the cancer, but my body was under too much stress.

I remained in ICU for five days. When I woke up, I realized that God had brought me through again—only I wasn't going to leave in two days. My hands were strapped to the bed, and a multitude of tubes and wires were hanging all over the place. I remained in the hospital for two and one-half weeks. My voice began to return after the first week.

My breathing was shallow due to a build-up of fluid in the lining of my lungs. I knew my recovery now would take some time. It was now three weeks before Pastors' School, and I was not sure I could pull through like the previous year.

I began to receive many cards and phone calls. I was not as optimistic about my recovery. I knew things were different. But God had not changed. The word was out that I was beginning to get stronger, but I had a long way to go.

Calvin had spent the last two weeks at my bedside without a good night's rest. I suggested that he drive home for the weekend. The children needed his encouragement that I was doing better, and he needed a well-deserved rest in his own bed. He agreed that it would be good to go home for a little while. I assured him that the nurses would take good care of me.

The following day my brother Mike and sister Laura walked into my room; it was such a surprise. They said that Dr. Schaap sent them to encourage me. I was overwhelmed with joy. It had seemed a rather lonely fight recovering from that surgery so far from home. We enjoyed the time together. We remembered many things from the past, and they updated me of the present things happening at home.

They could see that my breathing was still shallow. I told them that I had realized that God miraculously brought me through another surgery. I wanted them to know that the surgeons had kept me alive. I also told them that I was surrendered to the idea that my recovery might be long. I was not sure I could be ready to play my oboe for Pastors' School.

When my brother Mike told me he was singing the song "But I Have Prayed for Thee" during Pastors' School, I began to desire to play with him. He was a leader of one of the prayer groups, and the men were asked to open the conference with the song.

When I was first diagnosed with cancer, it took a week before Laura believed that I might be able to play my oboe during the conference. But this time she held a stronger faith. Then Laura got really excited and said, "Wouldn't that be neat! Just think all those people praying for you. And you would get to play that song."

I was so stirred by that thought that I began to desire to be there. That was when I began to have my faith increased. "Could God do it again?" I wondered.

The following weekend I was released to go home without oxygen. Though my breathing was much stronger, my strength was very limited. I was not eating well.

The next day I went to church. It was a challenge to be there. I have always believed that you will never know what you can do unless you try. Philippians 4:13 says, *"I can do all things through Christ which strengtheneth me."*

We had to return to Mayo the following week to discuss cancer treatments with Dr. Hartman, the oncologist. While I was there, the specialists removed fluid from my right side. I was able to breathe better. The doctor wanted me to understand that the treatment they were offering was my only hope. The doctor did not recommend any future surgeries with what I had gone through. "Also, if the cancer returns, it will probably hit the same area, but there isn't much left to attack," he added.

When I returned home while no one was around, I pulled out the oboe, but it took a lot of work to play. I went to the orchestra practice on the Saturday night before Pastors' School. I was able to play the important parts. I was not alone now. I had trained Amy Ossewaarde at the college with several lessons, and her diligence to learn brought her along quickly. She was the support that I needed.

The conference opened with Ron Hamilton singing the theme song "Bow the Knee." Later the men who had conducted our prayer groups came out and sang "But I Have Prayed for Thee." In the song Jesus came to Simon, knowing that Simon would go through a great trial, and Jesus assured Simon that He prayed for him. He wanted his faith not to fail; he would need to pray for others someday for them to have their faith not to fail. It is at this place in our lives we depend on others—when we are going through a great trial. Jesus was showing how we could help others—pray.

I played each night at Pastors' School. Each night the message was on prayer. I was too weak to sit for the long service, but I was able to do my part with the Lord's help.

After the conference I began my new chemo treatments. The doctors felt I was too weak to begin full strength. Each time I returned, the tumor mark reduced one third the amount. During the following months, my breathing improved as the fluid was gradually removed from the other lung.

If I had not the responsibility of playing the oboe, I would not have felt the obligation nor the drive to hurry and get well. After the first surgery, I feel that my playing my instrument provoked me to improve. Many friends were praying for me, and I did not want their prayers go unanswered. After the second surgery, I needed to rely more on the Lord than ever. God needed to do something big in order for me to play during the conference.

In May I went to our church's annual Mother and Daughter Banquet. I was delightfully surprised to receive the Overcomer Award. I would have to say that the great people of the First Baptist Church really earned this award. They are truly caring and praying people and are zealous of good works.

At my most recent visit at Mayo, I spoke with my oncologist. She hesitated and said, "I normally don't say this, but when I saw you in February 2007, I felt you only had a month to live." Her statement was a very sobering fact. We knew my condition was serious. She also mentioned, "I believe Somebody wanted you alive down here." She did not say directly that God wanted me here, but we knew she was referring to the Lord. My remarks were that a lot of people were praying for me. And in that month was the very important conference that I was to be playing my oboe.

When I was released from the ICU, I told her that I had told the Lord that I knew He had used Dr. Bobbi Gostout to preserve my life. I want to be grateful to the Lord for what He has done. I want to be a witness everywhere I go for him. He is a great God and worthy to be praised.

Fighting ovarian cancer will be a lifelong task. However long that may be, I want to live for Him. I did not fear that I had cancer. I just asked for His grace to fight the cancer. I know now after having two cancer surgeries that God has a definite appointment time for me to die. My appointment may be before yours or may be after yours. The question remains: "If you died today, would you go to Heaven?" If cancer knocked at your door, would you fear, or would your faith be increased that God is working a great work in your life?

The Brocks' Story
by Reed Brock

The year 2006 proved to be a very trying year for our family. The third week of May, my son went into the hospital with severe headaches. We were to believe that these headaches were the result of a malfunction of one of the two shunts he has. He would remain in the hospital for the entire week. While there, he was on very high doses of morphine with no relief at all for the first three days. The doctors performed all the routine examinations. After many drugs and shunt adjust-

The Reed Brock family

ments, on the fourth day we saw a change for the good in his condition. Eventually the pain subsided, and we were able to return home with David. Sort of scratching our heads, wondering exactly what had just happened, we lifted our hearts in praise to the Lord for once again being able to bring David home. Exhausted mentally and emotionally drained, we gave a sigh of relief, not knowing this was only a prelude of what was yet to come.

For many years my wife Bonnie has lived with a severe digestive disorder that rears its ugly head and causes episodes of excruciating pain if she even drinks something. This pain would literally bend her over, and she would spend the next few hours in this position. Prior to David's hospitalization, Bonnie was having one of those kind of weeks. Still, sick and bent over, she stayed night after night in the hospital with her son. The next week she spent totally bedridden, hurting too badly to be up or even drink some days. This episode lasted the entire next week after David came home from the hospital.

On the morning of June 1, 2006, I was in the kitchen cooking breakfast, and I asked David to go wake his mother for breakfast, hoping she could eat. David returned to the kitchen and very sheepishly said, "Dad, Mom said not to wake her up right now." Having been married to her for 31 years and watching her interact for the last 16 years with our children, I knew something was very wrong. I don't care how tired or how sick my wife was, when awakened by her children, she greeted them with an instant "I love you" and a hug.

I went into our bedroom and found her sleeping, I thought. I told her it was time to get up—no response. I leaned over and kissed her forehead and put my hand under the back of her neck. About that time, she gasped for air; her neck was stiff as if dead. She had suffered a severe stroke due to a blood clot. I called "911," and the paramedics responded quickly. Bonnie's blood pressure was 50/40, and the paramedics refused to transport her until her pressure was stabilized. However, it never stabilized, so they decided to carry her to the hospital anyway.

The next few hours were a total nightmare. I sat next to the table on which she was lying while the nurse assigned to her worked frantically to raise her blood pressure. All I could do was plead with God to let us keep her for just a while longer. She was placed on a breathing machine because the stroke had taken all body functions except the heartbeat, which, by the way, was surprisingly strong. For the next month and a half, she would be in a coma and not respond to anything.

Finally, one day she started trying to open her eyes. She began responding to certain people's voices as they visited with her. I was told she would be basically a vegetable the rest of her life.

But God in His graciousness allowed her to wake up, start talking, and just recently took three steps completely by herself. Praise God!!! At this time, she is still improving a little at a time, but she is improving.

"For the eyes of the LORD run to and fro throughout the whole earth, to shew himself strong in the behalf of them whose heart is perfect toward him...." (II Chronicles 16:9) Bonnie is now walking around our home with the assistance of a walking device and some very kind Christian ladies who have chosen to be used and to serve my wife. For this we are very thankful. God is good.

Meet More of My Friends...

Above: The Bob Hooker family
Below: The Sergio Garcia family

Meaghan's Story
by Janet Moore

M eaghan's story begins in October 1997. I had been sick for almost eight months when my doctor made a diagnosis for several of my symptoms: Graves' Disease, a rare disorder that affects the thyroid. My doctor explained to me that my immune system had suffered a severe trauma. She and her partners believe that a popular, doctor-prescribed diet aid that I had taken had caused this trauma.

Janet & Meaghan Moore

My doctor explained that I had hyperthyroidism; I felt a relief in finally knowing why I had been feeling the way I had been feeling for so long. She said that my blood levels indicated that I was very toxic. This explained why I had missed a few of my monthly cycles. I was given a couple of prescriptions. I specifically asked her if I needed to be careful about getting pregnant because of my diagnosis. She was very confident when she told me that even if I were to try to get pregnant, I would be unable to; and therefore, I should not be concerned about it. Unbeknownst to us, approximately two weeks later, Ron and I would conceive Meaghan.

On December 8, 1997, I was still very sick, and my symptoms seemed to be getting worse. The next evening my doctor told Ron and me that we were expecting. I told him that this was not possible and explained what I had been previously told by my endocrinologist. He explained that it was very rare to become pregnant when the body is in such a severe state of thyroid toxicity but that I was definitely pregnant.

On December 12, 1997, Ron went with me to my appointment with a high-risk pregnancy OB-GYN doctor. They explained to us that I would be seeing three of the doctors over the next seven months. After the doctor completed my examination, I was given a prescription for prenatal vitamins and an order for a couple of standard tests.

The doctor's office was in the hospital, so we went downstairs to the lab to have my blood drawn, and then we had the ultrasound done. It was incredible to see our baby so active and so full of life. I was happy that the technician kept taking so many extra measurements and pictures at different angles. It gave me more time to watch in awe as our child played before our eyes.

The next day the doctor's office called for us to come in. Then I started to feel uncomfortable about how long the technician had spent doing the ultrasound. We sat face to face with Dr. Lingren. He said that I needed to have some additional tests done, but he was quite sure of the results already. He just wanted to confirm them. He felt very strongly that our baby was physically deformed and would be severely mentally handicapped. He further informed us that upon the return of the results of the next set of tests, we needed to be prepared to terminate the pregnancy.

As soon as the words came out of his mouth, I knew that he had not just said what I had thought he said. I asked him to repeat himself. He informed me that based upon my previous tests, he was 97 percent sure that I would need to terminate my pregnancy.

At that point, I looked at my husband and told him to tell the doctor that abortion was not an option. The doctor became indignant and gave my husband and me a speech about neglect.

That night as I wrote to God in my journal, I told him that I trusted Him and His ways. I told Him that I knew that all of this was a part of His plan and that I was fine with whatever He wanted to do. I told God that I had never asked Him for a "perfect" child. I reminded Him of my friends with "special" children. I begged God to use this child for His glory. I told God that I knew He did not make mistakes. Then I thanked God for allowing me to be this child's mother. I reminded Him that I considered it a privilege to be used in the creation of another soul. Then, as with each of my pregnancies, I made my requests known to the Lord for specific traits that I would desire for this child. I asked God to remember that the desire of my heart was for this child to have my father's eyes for he has the most amazing eyes I have ever seen.

I wrote a note in my journal to my unborn child. I told my baby how blessed she was to be born into this family because she had the world's best daddy and the two best sisters anyone could ever have. I told her how excited everyone was that she was coming. I explained to her what the doctor had said. Then I told her that it did not matter what the doctor had said because God had made her just the way she was for a very special reason. Then I read Psalm 139 as I would so many times during this pregnancy.

At our next appointment, the doctor—seemingly almost proudly—confirmed that he was right. The test had confirmed that our baby, a girl, was physically and mentally deformed. Then he said, "Now with that knowledge, I am sure that you would like to discuss terminating this pregnancy. There is not a parent alive who would put a child through a short, limited life spent in the hospital connected to machines. That would not be financially wise either." With that, I actually smiled a real smile at him, and then Ron told him that we would be keeping him as our doctor through the FULL duration of my pregnancy.

This pregnancy was not an easy one. I was hospitalized 22 times over the next 6 months. Also, because my obstetrician had two other partners in his practice, I took turns seeing them. They wanted me to feel comfortable with each of them because whoever was on call when I went into labor would be the one who would deliver the baby.

I was not due to deliver until July 30. However, my health started to deteriorate, and on July 7, while at my **daily** doctor's appointment, they decided to admit me immediately to deliver. This was around 2:30 in the afternoon.

We did not know until 8:30 that evening which doctor would be performing my C-section. I was so excited when I saw Dr. Lingren walk through the doors. He was the doctor who had insisted we terminate this baby, and now he would deliver that same child. I knew that God was at work, and He was up to something.

At 10:30 that evening, I was taken into the operating room to administer my epidural. About 30 minutes later, they brought Ron and my sister-in-law Debra into the operating room to be with me. There were complications as they began. The doctor administered the fully allowed dosage into my epidural. It did not help much at all; I was in pain as they performed my C-section.

At 11:31 p.m., Meaghan Faith Moore was born, weighing 8 pounds 4 ounces and measuring 19½ inches long. I just kept asking, "How is she?" They immediately took her off to the side. I could hear them talking, but I could not understand what they were saying. I asked Ron to go over and see her. He left my side and went over to Meaghan's. He said, "Janet, she is perfect! I mean, she isn't deformed! There is nothing wrong with her!"

When the nurse gave Meaghan to Ron, he brought her over to me and opened her blanket. We counted her fingers, her toes, and turned her every which way. She looked at me, and I realized she was looking at me with my father's eyes! God had given me the desire of my heart. Her eyes were the exact same color as my dad's!

I said to Ron, "Please ask Dr. Lingren to come over here." He came over, and I asked him to hold her. Then I asked him to count her toes and fingers and check her over. He did so with a silly grin on his face. He then pointed out that she did indeed have a deformity—her tongue was attached all the way to the tip. He said that we needed to have it clipped now and that she would probably require speech therapy. We declined.

I was still very sick. Seventeen hours after Meaghan was born, my health took a turn for the worse. My friend, Stacey, was in my room with me, and I kept telling her that I felt like I was hyperventilating and like someone was sitting on my chest. I asked her to see if she could find a brown paper bag for me to breathe into. As I breathed in and out of the bag, to my dismay, I found no relief.

My mom and aunt were in the hallway with Stacey's mom, Sue. Ron was in my room trying to help me. Stacey went to the nurses' station to see what they thought. Just then, Dr. Roland walked into the room. She immediately said, "Hit the nurses' call button!" The only thing I remember from that point on is someone pushing me down the hall and putting a needle with a large syringe into my heart. It would be a little over a week before I would wake up.

When I did wake up, I was told that I was in the ICU of the hospital. I had suffered a *thyroid storm*. Four of my organs had shut down completely.

I asked about Meaghan and was told me she was perfectly fine in the nursery. Our pediatrician had made sure that she could stay in the hospital until I went home a week and a half later.

I had many opportunities to share my faith with others. It was amazing how many nurses and hospital employees came to my room to share with me that they had been praying for my family and me. I did not understand what they did—I was only the second person in the history of the hospital to survive a *thyroid storm*. Actually, it was not until my appointment with Dr. Roland a week after I was released from the hospital that I grasped the seriousness of it all. I asked her if I could have died. She became very serious as she explained to me that had she not walked into my hospital room when she did, I would have died right then and there.

As I write this, nine years have passed. Meaghan, who is now nine years old, is amazing. If you were to speak with her, you would agree that she speaks much better than most 13-year-olds. She enunciates her words beautifully, and her only birth defect has not held her back in any way.

When Meaghan was younger, we ran into Dr. Lingren. She asked him if he was the doctor who did not think it would be a great idea for us to have her. He was charmed immediately by her big, beautiful blue eyes and told her that surely he was mistaken.

Meaghan has been such a blessing to our family. She is always so excited and expressive about everything that we do. She loves and looks up to her older sisters in a very sweet manner. We truly cannot imagine these past nine years without her.

She makes friends everywhere she goes and points out the evidence of God to everyone she meets. I am always thrilled as she grabs a tract from my purse to give to someone she has just met. Meaghan trusted Christ as her Saviour when she was four years old. She will be in the fourth grade this fall. She is affectionately known as "Strawberry Shortcake" to those who know and love her.

In the book, *The Hiding Place*, by Corrie Ten Boom, Miss Ten Boom explains how her father helped her as a young child to understand the special grace that God gives us, even when facing death or the possibility thereof.

But that night as he stepped through the door, I burst into tears. "I need you!" I sobbed. "You can't die! You can't!"

Beside me on the bed Nollie sat up. "We went to see Mrs. Hoog," she explained. "Corrie didn't eat her supper or anything."

Father sat down on the edge of the narrow bed. "Corrie," he began gently, "when you and I go to Amsterdam—when do I give you your ticket?"

I sniffed a few times, considering this.

"Why, just before we get on the train."

"Exactly. And our wise Father in Heaven knows when we're going to need things, too. Don't run out ahead of Him, Corrie. When the time comes that some of us will have to die, you will look into your heart and find the strength you need—just in time."

(*The Hiding Place*, Corrie Ten Boom with John and Elizabeth Sherrill, 33)

———

Mr. Ten Boom's words were very wise. Since reading them, the Holy Spirit has brought them to my mind in times of anxiety. You know those times when you think ahead a little too far, wondering how we will handle different situations that are bound to come upon us sometime in our future. With each trial, decision, and heartache comes a measure of grace.

We as a family could truly see God's hand in it all. He was purging and shaping us as individuals and as a family unit. God was giving me an opportunity to do right. If He had not allowed me to be faced with this decision, I would not know the joy that I have today. I learned to make decisions based on Biblical principles. I am thankful that God trusted me with these choices.

Mrs. Moffitt is like a diamond. She has so many facets. She has the ability to give you hope for your future, forget your past hurts, and encourage you to love others. Each time I leave her presence I feel uplifted and desire to go give to others what I just received from her.

Brother and Mrs. Moffitt live for others. They eat, drink, and breathe others. If I am with them, on the phone with them, or hearing about them, *others* always come into the picture. They are constantly in the middle of helping others.

Our family has a very special affinity for the Moffitt family. They are our friends who are like family. They love on us and make us feel like we are one of them. The girls call Mrs. Moffitt, Grandma. The Moffitts are an addition to our lives, not a supplement.

Left: Ron and Janet Moore
Right: Todd Vaprezsan, Meaghan, and Joy Moffitt

Meet More of My Friends...

Above: The Tim McCurdy family
(Inset: Their son Clinton passed away February 5, 2006.)

Below left: Ron and Peggy Kendall

Below right: Tom and Jane Grafton

Meet More of My Friends...

Above: Dr. and Mrs. Jack Schaap and family
Below left: James and Evelyn Junkins
Below right: Frank and Linda Rechlicz
Page 119 above: The Tom Vogel family
Page 119 below: The Ray Young family

Meet More of My Friends...

Meet More of My Friends...

Above:
The Dennis Kelly family

Below left:
The Mike Krystyn family

Below right:
Miss Vicky Siebenhaar

Meet More of My Friends...

Above left: Miss June Ryland
Above center: Miss Lynette Stroud
Above right: Miss Joan Lindish

Below:
Marcia and Sheldon Schearer

Meet More of My Friends...

Steve and Pat McPherson

(Steve passed away in February 2007.)

My buddies and my friends: Gabrielle, Victoria, and Madison Wonson

Part II—Join Me in Discovering Ways to Find Even More Joy!

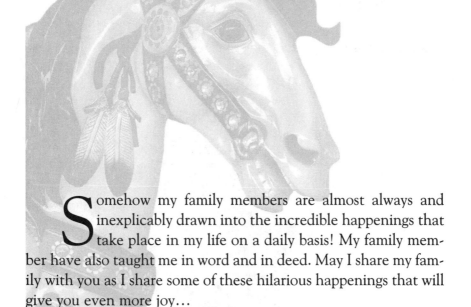

Somehow my family members are almost always and inexplicably drawn into the incredible happenings that take place in my life on a daily basis! My family member have also taught me in word and in deed. May I share my family with you as I share some of these hilarious happenings that will give you even more joy…

What I Didn't Learn
in Finishing School

Many years ago I worked in professional modeling and actually taught at the Patricia Stevens Modeling and Finishing School. After I started working for First Baptist Church, I wondered if I'd ever be able to use that training again. Shortly before I transferred to work at Hyles-Anderson College, Mrs. Marlene Evans, the Dean of Women, asked me to come and speak to the girls' split chapel to teach the young ladies some tips on proper ladylike dress.

I was so excited to share with the young ladies some ideas on how to dress and to give some pointers on how to sit and stand like a lady. I carefully chose my clothes for that morning and even decided to wear my brand new expensive heels for the first time. As I started to leave for chapel, I remembered, "Oh, I'm driving the car that always ruins my right heel because of the worn-out rug under the gas pedal. I'll ruin my new heels! I know, I'll take along my old run-down heels and just put the old right heel on to drive to the college. Then I will change to the new heel after I arrive. That will take care of the problem perfectly!"

I became totally engrossed in reviewing my teaching notes in my mind as I drove, and I forgot I had my new heel on my left foot and the old ugly one on my right foot. I pulled up to the front of the college and parked in the visitor space. I prayed for the Lord to bless my talk, and I went on my way into the school. I was escorted to a waiting area along with another lady who was also a former professional model.

As we waited to be escorted in to speak, she said to me in a very feminine and caring way, "JoJo, do you know that you have two different heels on?"

I just yelped, "Oh no!" and related to her, Mrs. Evans, and Mrs. Evans' secretary (who graciously went and retrieved my shoe from my car) what had happened. Yes, how wonderful it was that only four of us knew about my mix-up.

But that relief didn't last long. As soon as we were introduced, Mrs. Evans just had to tell all the college girls about my near "tragedy" that had happened just before that split chapel service. The story surely helped to break the ice as well as to give all of us a good healthy laugh. I promise you, I may have worn two different earrings a time or two, but I have never messed up my shoes since then!

Teachings

1. Be willing to laugh at your "boo-boos" when you mess up.
2. If you ever decide to get a little proud, realize that God will humble you quickly.
3. How simple it would have been to replace the old, damaged carpeting with a new piece!
4. When someone points out a flaw, learn from it and be grateful by sincerely saying, "Thank you."
5. Never appear to be a "Miss Priss." Learn to be transparent and touchable.

"By humility and the fear of the LORD are riches,
and honour, and life." (Proverbs 22:4)

Above: JoJo as Miss City of Whiting in 1964

JoJo with her modeling partner, Pam, doing an ad for the **Chicago Tribune** newspaper. This is Cuddley Duddley, the **Tribune** mascot.

Above left: A modeling job in 1966

Above right: Cleopatra "JoJo" at the McCormick Place in Chicago, Illinois, in 1966.

Miss Wembley (JoJo Moffitt) doing promotional advertising for Wembley neckties and Arrow shirts for men at the old E. C. Minas Store in Hammond, Indiana.

A smile is contagious, so pass it on.

Please, I Need a Razor!

Recently while I was out of town, I decided to unpack my bag first thing and make myself right at home in my motel room. I realized as I was unpacking my toiletry bag that I had forgotten one important item—my shaver. "No problem," I thought. Right there before my eyes in the bathroom was a little sign, "In case you forgot any toiletry item, please call the front desk, and we will meet your need." Wow! A direct answer to prayer, and it's right before my eyes.

I immediately went to the phone to place the call, but in the process, I forgot about my suitcase on the floor, and I tripped over it. Boy, did I take a fall. I dialed 0, and the operator answered, "Yes, ma'am, Mrs. Moffitt, may we help you?" How unbelievable, they call you by name.

Because of the fall, I was still quite out of breath. In a very heavy, labored tone, I said, "Sir, I need a razor!"

He said, "A razor?"

"Yes, I need a razor in Room 232."

He seemed concerned by my voice tones, which I'm sure sounded almost distraught. "Ma'am, why do you need a razor?"

"Sir, I need a razor, and I need it badly."

He said, "Ma'am, maybe we need to talk?" I'm sure this guy thought I was going to slit my wrists; I kid you not.

I said, "Sir, is there a reason why you feel I shouldn't have a simple razor?"

"Ma'am, everything is going to be okay. Why don't you take a short nap and rest a while? Would you like one of our female employees to come up and be with you at this time?"

"Sir, I'm fine. I just fell over my suitcase, and that is why I'm out of breath and possibly appear to be in pain. Please may I just have a razor?"

He finally sent up an employee with the razor, some cookies, and a warm cup of tea. Wow! What you have to go through to get a complimentary razor!

As I continued on my way, I decided to use the new razor. Can you believe it? Yes, it happened. I'm now running close to time to leave the motel, and I'm late in getting ready. The unthinkable happened—I cut my leg.

Because my platelets are low, I bled for almost five minutes. What a mess! I now have toilet tissue stuck to my leg, taking the place of a bandage. I'm not about to call the front desk because I just know they'll send up the "special employees" who man the straight jacket, and I'll be off to the mental ward. All this because I forgot my razor?!

I really got tickled as I relived the whole situation. Maybe I should have listened to the man at the front desk in the first place. It was obvious I couldn't be trusted with a razor.

Teachings

1. Unpack your suitcase in a safe area. How about the bed or the dresser?
2. Take extra razors with you when you travel.
3. If you travel by air, trust me; pack them in your checked suitcase and don't carry them in your purse. If you forget and leave them in your purse, you will have them taken from you, or you might be able to write your "razor story" from jail.

4. If concerned, check and see if they have extra-sensitive, extra-safe, kid-proof razors next time you make a purchase.
5. Use Nair—it removes unwanted hair!

"Trust in the LORD with all thine heart; and lean not unto thine own understanding. In all thy ways acknowledge him, and he shall direct thy paths." (Proverbs 3:5-6)

Meet More of My Family...

Above: My brother and sister-in-law, Jim and Lynn Kinnane,
and their grandchildren

Below left to right: My sister, Cindy Balko; her children, Katie, Tim,
and Karen; and my brother-in-law, Tim Balko

It is your responsibility to create joy.

Hey, Doctor, Will You Please Pray?

Before I had surgery a few years ago, I warned my doctor, Dr. Jack Schwartz, that I was a "rare bird." I made a believer of him by the end of the whole ordeal. After my going through a minor procedure, my doctor would determine whether or not I would need to have a complete hysterectomy. I told my doctor beforehand not to wake me up to ask permission if there were problems but to go ahead and just care for the problem completely. He followed my wishes and did just that.

When I woke up, I was thinking I'd get to go home that afternoon from having a simple laparoscopic exploratory procedure. I remember thinking to myself, "I think they left all the tools in me. Is this how you really feel after this simple procedure?"

I did not realize that the laparoscopy would reveal some major concerns. Not only did I need to have a complete hysterectomy, I also needed a repair for a rectocele and a cystocele, as well as a repair of the colon. Needless to say, I was quite sore. I was almost relieved to know it was more serious because I felt like a baby at first from the discomfort of a "simple" test.

On day two, what should have been minor became even more major. The small incision near my navel through which the doctors go in with the scope ruptured. I had just gotten freshened up for the day and was attempting to walk in my room when blood started pouring out of the incision. I put my finger in "the dike" to stop the bleeding. A nursed entered as I said, "I think I have a problem?!" She heartily agreed and quickly called the doctor. In minutes he was on site. The doctor was just about to cauterize the area when I said, "Stop!"

"What?!"

I said, "Stop!"

He looked stunned at this time. I needed some break in the atmosphere, so, of course, I used humor. (Please realize that when I was a child, I asked my dad why I had that hole in the middle of my tummy. He jokingly told me it was where the Indian shot me—I thought he was serious. "Why did the Indian shoot me there?" I wondered.)

"Doctor," I said, "are you going to put that pointed object into my navel?"

"Yes," he replied, " if it will stop the bleeding."

I thought, "Oh no, that's where the Indian shot me!" Before I knew it, I said, "Wait! If I live through this, I'm going to medical school to become a navel specialist, and I'm coming after you."

All the folks in the room laughed—the doctor, two nurses, and my husband. The only person not really laughing was me. The doctor was laughing so hard his hand was shaking, and he was about to come after me! The situation really was funny.

But it didn't stop there. Two more times I began bleeding and had to go back for repairs. During my last office visit, I underwent another test only to discover I now had a bowel blockage. To understand the seriousness of my situation, you have to realize that my blood count was very low, and I would need a transfusion to make it through another surgery. Also, a bowel procedure would have been more complicated because of my kidney disease.

As I was leaving the doctor's office for the fourth time, I looked at my doctor and said, "Hey, Dr. Schwartz, would you please pray that it's not a blockage?" He agreed to do so. After having the special testing at the hospital, we left for home. I asked my husband, "Is Brother Hyles in town?" I just felt I'd be okay if we could see him and have him pray with us. On our way home, we stopped by our church around 8:00 in the evening, and sure enough, he was still there.

He graciously came out and prayed a prayer that went something like this: "Dear God, we sure wish we could heal JoJo, but we can't. Please, Lord, meet the needs she has right now. We are asking You if it be Your will, please help

Dr. and Mrs. Jack Hyles

in the matter of what could be a blockage. She will serve You, Lord, however You choose, but she could serve You much greater if her health were restored." (Please realize I could never repeat his exact prayer, but I believe it was similar to what I've written.)

I still remember how weak I was. I could hardly walk—much less even climb up our stairs.

As soon as we arrived home, the phone rang. You know who it was, don't you? It was our wonderful, caring doctor. He said, "JoJo, did you pray?"

I thought, "That's funny—that's the last thing I asked him to do," so I said, "Yes, doctor, I did. Did you?"

He said, "I sure did. You won't believe it."

I thought, "Oh, yes I will!"

"There is no blockage!"

We all cried and rejoiced together. He now agrees that I'm a "rare bird." God is so good. He's given me more time and more time to keep the promise I made years ago. May I share that promise with you?

"Whatever time I have, Lord, it's Yours." That is a promise I will keep, and I renew it every day of my life. I'm thankful daily that He's given me more time to serve Him and His people. I'm especially thankful to precious doctors who have been more than doctors to me; they are my friends. Along with the Lord's help, many doctors are responsible for my being alive today.

Teachings

1. Keep your spirits up even during the "down times."
2. Prayer works. Just keep on praying till light breaks through. Just keep on praying; He'll answer you and me, too.
3. Be a walking testimony to others, especially during your testing times in life.
4. When you give your life to the Lord, He gives you more life in return.
5. The Indian really never shot me, just in case you're wondering. (Psst, a secret—it's called a navel.)

———

"But rejoice, inasmuch as ye are partakers of Christ's sufferings; that, when his glory shall be revealed, ye may be glad also with exceeding joy." (I Peter 4:13)

Do You Know Your
License Plate Number?

Many years ago we used to own an old, well-used 1986 Plymouth Voyager van. There is no way I can express how useful this van was, especially on the weekends picking up bus riders for church. We also loved it on vacations since we could take it on long trips. We could remove the center seat for the kids to "camp out," as we put foam mats and heavy sleeping bags there. They used the space to sleep and play as we traveled on a long journey.

Well, my old, treasured van took a beating. We decided in class at Hyles-Anderson College to plan a "baby shower by air" for Joy and Jeff Ryder, the daughter and son-in-law of Dr. Wendell Evans, the president of Hyles-Anderson College. Since they were serving as missionaries in New Guinea, we knew they could use almost anything for their new baby. We decided to have a money shower for them. With the money we collected, I then purchased all the baby goods.

I drove over to Venture, a local department store that was in our area, and had the time of my life. I found diapers, sleepers, blankets, sheets, shoes, socks, clothes, T-shirts, toys, a fold-up stroller, bed, infant seat, powder, shampoo, safety pins, lotion, diaper bag, baby bottles, booties, brush, pacifiers, bibs, spoons, cups, plates, blue and pink streamers, "It's a girl!" and "It's a boy!" plastic banners (since we didn't know what she was going to have), and a few things for Joy of a personal nature. We carefully packed all these gifts to send to New Guinea where they were actually dropped by air near the Ryder's remote location. It truly was a "baby shower by air."

It was so much fun shopping until I heard the announcement over the P.A. system, "Would the owner of a van, license plate number 94C9634, please come to the service desk."

I thought, "Oh, I guess someone left their lights on—too bad!" I went back to shopping.

Again I heard the announcement, "If you are the owner of a gray Plymouth Voyager van, license plate number 94C9634, it is vital that you come immediately to the service desk. Your car has been in an accident!"

I quickly thought, "Van...I have a van! License plate number what? I know my house number, my social security number, my phone number, but my license plate number...no way! An accident, it can't be my van. My van is parked. How could it drive off and get into an accident? I have the keys. Oh well, I'd better check it out."

I got to the service desk just as the lady making the report was leaving. The lady appeared very shaken and was crying hard. I stopped her and asked her what had happened. She pointed out to the parking lot. Sure enough, she had turned in too closely with her husband's prized possession, a 1956 restored Chevrolet, and had sideswiped the entire side of my van.

I thought, "She is so shaken up. She is more important than an old piece of metal. How can I help and comfort her?"

I told her I would need to call the police to make a report, and she literally sobbed, "My husband is going to kill me!"

I thought, "There doesn't even appear to be a dent in her heavy car, and mine could easily be repaired. God, You allowed this to happen for a reason." I tried to comfort her as we made our report. She had wonderful insurance coverage. She told me she was a physicist, so surely money was not a problem.

As we walked back toward Venture and entered the area where the announcement had been made, I made this brilliant statement, "This is no ACCIDENT that we met." I then got tickled, and so did she.

We definitely met by accident that day. I stopped right there and said, "You didn't hit me on purpose, did you? There is a reason we've met." I then asked her if she knew for sure she was on her way to Heaven. When she said "no," I took out my New Testament and showed her how she could know for sure she was on her way to Heaven. Within minutes she bowed her head and prayed and asked Jesus to be her Saviour and her only way to Heaven. We hugged, and she went on her way. I wish you could have seen the folks at the service desk looking at us so confused.

A few days later my husband and I took some paperwork to her home. Her grateful husband thanked us over and over again for helping his wife. My husband then shared how he, too, could know for sure he was on his way to Heaven, and he also trusted Christ.

What we didn't know was that that lady, although very intelligent and wealthy, had just been out of the hospital a few days after suffering a nervous breakdown and truly needed some compassion and love. It made me more conscious of a statement Brother Hyles used to share, "Be good to everybody because everybody's having a tough time."

I learned many lessons from this experience, but one I learned for sure is that I need to memorize my license plate number. (When I get it renewed, I always choose a simple one to remember.) Don't forget; I'm almost a senior citizen. I turned 61 years old on July 23, 2007, and I'm still alive! Yippee!

Teachings

1. Don't hurt people; instead, go out of your way to help them.
2. If you see a need, go meet it; don't expect someone else to do it.
3. Be a testimony during the testing and trial times.
4. Realize you can be a blessing or a cursing. The choice is yours and mine too.
5. Realize nothing happens "by accident." Learn from all God allows into your path. Always have joy and show it.

———

"Strengthened with all might, according to his glorious power, unto all patience and longsuffering with joyfulness."
(Colossians 1:11)

Remember God Loves You, and He Makes No Mistakes

In November quite a few years ago, I started having really bad sinus problems. If you lived in this area, you would understand. I tease that we live in "Soot City." I was born and reared in the Indiana area near the oil refineries and steel mills. With all the industry around here, naturally we have concern with pollution. It's easy to end up with allergies and sinus problems. I never had them though, until just a couple years ago when I had pneumonia. It just seemed like my whole system changed a bit. I became very susceptible to colds and infections.

This sinus problem continued on into December and even into January. I thought, "Boy this is crazy. We just can't seem to beat this. Something is really wrong." I decided to go see Dr. Dennis Streeter, a close family friend and an excellent doctor. I knew he'd find the underlying cause.

"Dr. Dennis," I said, "I don't know why, but I'm just getting so run down." He was so good. He prescribed some vitamins and even some vitamin shots.

"You know," I continued, "something just doesn't seem to be right in me. Everything seems to be just *off* a little bit in my system."

He said to me, "Well, what do you mean?"

I replied, "I'm so tired and just not myself."

"Well, let me just run a test."

"What kind of test?" I asked.

"A pregnancy test," he replied.

"A pregnancy test for sinus problems? No, no, we don't need this," I exclaimed. You have to understand. Our children were fifteen, twelve, and nine at the time. I just couldn't believe I was pregnant. So I said, "Okay, if you want to do this, it will be fine. Go ahead," and kind of laughed. I thought, "Boy, is he in for a surprise."

So he ran the test on Tuesday and said, "I'll call you Wednesday with the results."

I started to get tickled. I thought, "What? Me pregnant? Pregnant—that's like Sarah and Abraham!" I said to myself again, "I'm not pregnant. I just have a sinus infection. I'm just stuffed up."

Truthfully, I was a little bit concerned that maybe they'd find something seriously wrong with me. Each time the phone rang, I picked up the phone because I was anxiously waiting for the test results.

True to his word, Dr. Streeter called about 5:50 Wednesday evening. I'll never forget that call as long as I live. He said, "JoJo, this is Dr. Dennis Streeter."

I said, "Yes, Sir, how are you doing?"

He countered, "How are you feeling?"

I said, "Boy, I'm still so blocked up."

"You're going to be blocked up—for nine months!"

"What do you mean?" I asked. I thought he was joking; after all, he is a friend of ours. I thought, "Pregnant?"

My husband was sitting in the family room. He had just come home from work at the church. My husband is an assistant pastor at the church, and he comes home a little later on Wednesday before church, eats quickly, and then off he goes back to the church for teachers' meeting a short time later. I pulled the phone from the kitchen to the dining room where Roy couldn't hear—like I was going to keep pregnancy a secret or something. My emotions were so mixed up and confused. I cannot explain how I felt.

I said, "Would you explain that again?"

He repeated, "You're going to be 'blocked up' for the next nine months."

"I'm pregnant? You *are* kidding me."

He started laughing, "No, I'm not kidding you. You're three months pregnant."

His news truly came as a shock to me. "A baby?" I said incredulously I started to cry; then I started to laugh, and then I didn't know if I should cry and laugh together. Oh, I was confused, so I said, "Could you tell Roy for me?"

He said, "Sure." By this time, Dr. Streeter was getting tickled.

Roy was in the family room, so I walked in and said, "Roy, it's Dr. Streeter. Could you talk to him for just a minute?" I can't imagine what Roy must have thought, maybe that I had leukemia or something very, very serious by the look on my face. I handed him the phone, and I went and hid in the bathroom. I don't even know why I hid in the bathroom. I was so excited, but I was also embarrassed by the fact that I was crying and laughing and then crying again.

My reaction was disbelief. "You're kidding, really? Are you sure? Are you telling me the truth? Is this a joke? Is this true?" Then I started crying. I handed Roy the phone, and his reaction was, "You're kidding. Ha! Ha! I don't believe it. Ha! Ha! Ha!"

I thought, "He's laughing. I'm crying. Oh, no." What mixed emotions we had! We didn't have time to really talk before he left except that I said, "Roy, I'm pregnant."

He said, "I know, Honey. After all these years, isn't this tremendous?"

I said, "Yeaaaahh." Now I'm crying like a baby. "Let's not tell anyone. Don't tell anyone—nobody at all."

He said, "Okay, we won't tell anybody."

Then I said, "We'll tell the kids first, but they can't tell anyone, okay?"

"Okay, we won't tell anyone," he replied again.

"Okay, fine, promise me you won't tell anybody." We went through this conversation for another 20 minutes or so, back and forth…but I never told him I wouldn't tell anyone.

We got into the car and told the kids. You wouldn't believe the expressions on their faces. They all thought it was a joke, too. They said, "Oh, Mom, really?" Remember the kids are older—fifteen, twelve, and nine. Oh, they became excited. We were already choosing names before we got to church. Also by the time we got to church, we had decided that we were going to tell people that I was pregnant. My husband then announced it that night in the bus meeting. He just absolutely announced to everyone who would listen that we were going to have a baby in August. Roy told Brother Hyles, and he was excited and rejoiced with us. To say the least, people were thrilled to death! I mean, at first we weren't going to tell anyone, but we ended up telling the whole church. People couldn't believe it, but boy, were they excited.

Dr. Streeter saw Roy and kind of looked at him funny when he announced it. I'll never forget this, and I wondered why he wasn't excited with us. Although I felt I had just had the sinus problem, I think he was just concerned that I was in good health. It wasn't that he wasn't excited, but he was wise.

That was Wednesday night. The next morning Mrs. Evans announced in split chapel at the college that I was going to have a baby. The girls excitedly yelled and clapped. Of course, my news spread through the college because I worked with Mrs. Evans as an assistant teacher.

You know how when something exciting happens, you want to tell the whole world? You know what I found out? It's good to tell, but sometimes it is better to wait. You weigh the situation and think, "Well, why not? If you have some exciting, happy news, share it."

By Saturday we were already out looking for furniture and picking out baby clothes. I'm serious. We went out and purchased a pink dress. Pat Hayes, a lady with whom I worked, bought the most beautiful pink ruffled dress with a pink frilly bow in the back. The names we chose were "Jason James" and "Joy Marlene." We chose "Jason" for the manly name it is, and the name "James" after my dad, my brother, and my husband's brother. I love the name "Joy" (in honor of Joy Evans Ryder), and the middle name "Marlene" was of course for Mrs. Evans.

On Sunday as I was getting ready for church, I was already wanting to wear maternity clothes. I wasn't even showing, but I wanted everyone to know I was pregnant. On Monday I went to the college. I remember feeling very tired, very sleepy, and drained of energy that day. I usually left the college around 4:30 p.m.; but at 3:50 p.m., I was experiencing unusual stomach cramps.

Have you ever sensed there was a problem and found out later you were right? I realized that something was wrong, so I called my obstetrician, Dr. Carolyn Rawlins, and she ordered two different medications to help with the situation. I followed everything she suggested explicitly. I remember how I clung to the Lord and said, "Lord, please don't take this baby. Please don't take my child. Oh, Lord, please don't let anything happen to this baby. Please, please, please, don't let me lose my baby."

The next few hours were such a lonely time for me. Dr. Rawlins ordered me to stay off my feet the next day, and the discomfort had subsided by the end of the day. Some friends came to help me with duties around the house.

A little bit before 5:00 p.m., my husband left to go get some groceries. My sister Cindy came to visit, and while she was there, I started experiencing severe cramping. Something frightening happened within my body, and I felt I was about to lose the baby. I will never forget how glad I was that my sister was with me.

When Roy came home, I told him what had happened and he called Dr. Streeter. God was in control because that night Dr. Streeter had evening hours, and was there for us. He instructed us to come to his office so he could check out the situation. I can still remember what he said after he performed the examination. "If you haven't lost the baby, you will in the next few hours, JoJo."

I remember leaving without saying much, and just quietly sitting in the car. I'll never forget going home, walking into the house, facing our three children, and telling them the news. My mom, my in-laws, and my sister were all there waiting. They were there to rejoice with me about my pregnancy, but instead we ended up crying together.

Within a few hours, our baby passed away. But it didn't stop there. I had another checkup and learned that I was seriously ill with a severe infection. I was admitted to the hospital because toxins had built up in my system.

Although this time could have been very discouraging for me, I remember crying out to the Lord. I felt so alone and so lonely. But God taught me, trained me, and gave me time to rest.
I read the Bible and learned to love Him more. I also renewed my vows of giving my life full time to the Lord in being the right kind of wife, mother, and Christian worker. One especially hard night, the words of Psalm 30:5 became very real to me. "*...Weeping may endure for a night, but joy cometh in the morning.*"

During this time I found out that Pat Waters, a friend of mine in South Carolina, was having surgery. In fact, doctors had just diagnosed her with Hodgkin's Disease, a form of cancer. Pat, who was a bus kid from First Baptist Church was now married with four children, had faithfully worked on my bus route. When I learned that she had cancer, my heart broke. I called Pat because I wanted so much to encourage her heart, but I'll never forget what an encouragement she was to me.

As soon as she answered the phone in the hospital, she said, "Oh, Mrs. Moffitt, I just need to talk to you."

I thought, "Oh, Lord, thank You. Maybe I'll be able to help somebody."

She said, "Please call me back." The nurse was with her, and preparations were being made for her surgery the next day.

I said, "I sure will, Pat."

I did call her back, and she again said, "I need to talk to you. I heard you lost your baby."

Can you believe that? She was facing surgery to have her cancerous spleen removed, and she was concerned about me. Then she said something to me I'll never forget. "Oh excuse me, you didn't lose your baby. The Lord looked down and said, 'I need a little baby up here to love right now. I want a special baby. He looked all over and saw a special couple named the Moffitts. They're going to have that special baby.' So the Lord just reached down and took the little baby in His arms and took it to Heaven."

Oh, what an encouragement her words were! I realized anew that God is good. He loves us. He makes no mistakes. I decided then that I wasn't going to go through this trial and miss what the Lord wanted me to learn during this hard time. I can't really care until I've first been there. I'm glad I've been there. I can't wait to get to Heaven and meet my precious child waiting for me.

Don't miss being an encouragement and a blessing. May we each desire to be a blessing. "Make me a blessing, Make me a blessing—Out of my life may Jesus shine; Make me a blessing, O Saviour, I pray, Make me a blessing to someone today."

Teachings

1. I have a perfect child waiting for me in Heaven. Heaven is a wonderful place. Who is waiting for you?
2. Turn your sorrows into joy. Never lose your joy.
3. Cherish your children; cherish being their mom.
4. Never take anyone or anything for granted.
5. Turn the loss of a child into a ministry and meet the needs of someone going through the same thing. Run to that person's rescue. Call them on the phone, send flowers, take a meal, offer to run errands, clean their house, baby-sit for their other children, or just go by and say, "I care. I love you and your family."

———

"For his anger endureth but a moment; in his favour is life:
weeping may endure for a night, but joy cometh in the morning."
(Psalm 30:5)

Hey, You With the Big Shoes; Get Off the Floor!

I still remember back in grade school when I appeared "different" from my friends, and I didn't want to be that way *at all*. When I was in the eighth grade at Sacred Heart School in Whiting, Indiana, I still remember two exciting happenings in my life that year. First, I was chosen to be Bernadette in the school operetta. (Bernadette was nothing like me. She was small, frail, and very pale.) Secondly, I made the cheerleading squad and absolutely loved it! The only problem with these two honors was being told that I had to wear my corrective shoes wherever I went.

My dad tried to convince me that my shoes were great, but I knew better. These heavy, **ugly**, clunky shoes were also known as "saddle shoes." I could barely lift my feet off the ground, let alone cheer while wearing them! How could I possibly meet my cheerleading responsibilities with them on?

One day I discovered how to get by without wearing my saddle shoes. I told my dad I'd wear them, and I did. But...I only wore them to the corner.

Me at age eight

— 149 —

As soon as I reached the high bushes one block away from my house, I changed into my "good" shoes that I had hidden there. I carefully hid the hated saddle shoes in the bushes; and after school, I changed back into them so my dad would not be angry at me.

However, our inquisitive neighbor named Mrs. Gorman saw me being sneaky and decided it was her duty to call my dad and advise him about my actions. The next day was a basketball game, so I dressed in my uniform and respectfully put on my saddle shoes. As soon as I got to the corner, I changed into my white tennis shoes for the game.

What I didn't know was that my dad had followed me and watched exactly what I was doing. After school I happened to look out into the excited, waiting crowd and was stunned when I spotted my dad. He motioned for me to come to him. "Where are your corrective shoes?" he asked. I could tell by the look on his face that I had disappointed him.

I just looked down in embarrassment. Earlier in the day he had found my shoes in their hiding place and had brought them with him. He handed them to me and said, "What do you plan to do with these?"

I sat down and put on my corrective shoes. Then I ran—as fast as I could run in those shoes—out on the floor. The shoes felt like two 100-pound people sitting on my feet!

As I ran onto the floor and began the cheer, the referee stopped the cheer with a loud whistle. We all stopped immediately. He looked at me and said, "Hey, you, with the big shoes. Get off the floor! You're scratching our newly reconditioned floor."

I was embarrassed by the referee's words, but not nearly as embarrassed and hurt as when I saw my dad's disappointed face. To this day I gasp when I see corrective shoes, and I still run when I see bushes. (Just kidding!) I wore those shoes to please and to obey my dad, and because of my desire to please my dad, I reaped another benefit—my feet have been straight these many years. I'm glad I had a caring, loving, and consistent dad. How much better everything works out when we trust and obey.

And the moral of the story is...*Father knows best. Do what he says, and hang the rest.*

Teachings

1. Realize Mom and Dad always know what is best.
2. Obey without delay.
3. Honor your mom and dad all the days of your life.
4. If you have to wear corrective shoes, pad the bottoms with cotton. (Ha! Ha! just kidding)
5. Cheer on through the wins and losses in life.

————

"Children, obey your parents in the Lord: for this is right. Honour thy father and mother; which is the first commandment with promise; That it may be well with thee, and thou mayest live long on the earth." (Ephesians 6:1-3)

LEFT TO RIGHT: Mrs. Charles W. Fett, President, Whiting Junior Women's Club; JoJo Kinnane, recipient; Judge William Obermiller; Mrs. Thomas Hussey, President-elect

Present Outstanding Teen-Ager Of The Year Awards

Monday night, June 1st, Miss Anita "Jo Jo" Kinnane was presented a trophy and other gifts as the Outstanding Teen-Ager of the Year. The residents of the Whiting-Robertsdale area were asked to submit letters explaining why their particular choice should be awarded the title of Outstanding Teen-Ager of the year. These letters were turned over to an impartial panel of judges who made the final selection. "Jo Jo" is truly an Outstanding Teen-Ager in that she is active in community affairs, school affairs, church and helps in the family business. She is known in the community for her winning smile, her kindness to young and old alike, she works in a supermart part time and also does babysitting. Other awards which Jo Jo has received in the past year are as follows:

1963-64 Whiting High School Homecoming Queen, Ideal Senior, Friendliest, Kampus Kate award, GAC Trophy, Scholarship "W."

She is active in many school and local activities: Secretary of Sacred Heart CYO, Editor of Hammond Times Youth Column, Page Editor for school newspaper, head of PomPom Girls, "The Oilerettes," member of Honor Band and Senior High Band, Booster Club President, member of GAC, Girls Club, Booster Club, Spanish Club, FTA, member of Whiting Sub-Juniors.

Among the many things that Jo Jo can be proud of is her attendance record in school is exceptional. Jo Jo has had perfect attendance for her full 12 years in school. She graduated from Whiting High School on June 3 and plans to attend Indiana University in the fall.

Judge Obermiller presented the trophy to Jo Jo and Mrs. Charles Fett presented the other awards. The Contest was sponsored by the Whiting Junior Woman's Club.

Down But Not Out

I will never forget the time I took a "cool" but embarrassing fall right in front of my entire family. I had just finished preparing dinner that night when I realized I still had two hours before we needed to leave for the Wednesday night Bible study. While they were still eating, I decided to go out to our backyard and skim the leaves off our pool. With everyone watching me through the window, I waved to them and went to work.

I had been outside for only a few minutes when one of our neighbors started to visit with me from across the yard. Realize now, I was all dressed for church. I was wearing a church dress, heels, and jewelry when the usual drama in my life began. As I turned to answer my neighbor, John Marinakos, I lost my footing at the shallow end of the pool. Before I knew it—splash! I fell in and was drenched from head to toe. I was so embarrassed.

I quickly thought to myself, "I can beat this by drowning, or I'll be a big girl, walk to the stairs, climb up the two stairs, and walk out." You guessed it! I decided against drowning. I thought, "I'll just walk up the stairs and out of the water like nothing happened. I'm sure no one will say anything." Right!!!!

As I reached solid ground, my neighbor just couldn't resist saying, "JoJo, what were you doing?"

I answered quickly, "Oh, I was just a little warm and thought I'd take a quick dip before church." Warm is right! My face was beet red! Walking into our home and seeing my family laughing uncontrollably made me start laughing, too.

Realize you *will* goof up. Learn to laugh at yourself during these times. When you fall, get up quickly and move on.

And the moral of the story is…Don't let anything keep you down. Get up and go again and again and again and….

Teachings

1. Realize the times you remember most are the tough times.
2. Learn to laugh at yourself over and over again.
3. The Bible says, *"A merry heart doeth good like a medicine…."* Have you taken your medicine today?
4. Don't skim your pool. Just let the leaves float and enjoy them. (HA! Just kidding!)
5. Remember, you may fall down, but you're not out. Get up and go again.

———

"For a just man falleth seven times, and riseth up again: but the wicked shall fall into mischief." (Proverbs 24:16)

The Roy Moffitt family, Christmas 2005

No one can take away your joy but you.

I'm Falling,
But I Must Get Up!

When each of our six children was about ten months old, my husband and I would start to watch for each of them take their first steps in life. I remember how thrilled we were, how we clapped loudly, and how we cheered them on. But as we get older, we adults sometimes forget and do not think before we put *our* feet into action.

Our son, Mike Moffitt, who is now a police officer

When I was in my last month of pregnancy carrying Justin, I decided to ride the 45 minutes with my husband to our son Mike's wrestling match. I thought if I went into labor, at least we will be together!

When we arrived at the wrestling match, we parked right in front of the gym and went in to watch the event. It seemed quite unusual to find such a good parking place. (What we didn't know was that the parking spot we had used was reserved for the pastor of the church. Snow had covered the reserved signs.) Inside the gym the tournament was in progress. Three matches were going on at the same time. I knew it was really important for us to sit in the correct section so I could see and also let Mike know that I was cheering for him. But just as I sat down in the center section where he was supposed to be wrestling, a forfeit caused my son's match to be moved to another mat.

I thought, "Oh no, now what do I do? As large as I am, I can't climb down through all these people. I know me, I'll probably trip." I was on the third tier of the bleachers, so I decided just to sit there and enjoy the match.

However, before Mike's match was to begin, I realized that I couldn't see at all. The view to my left where the match was being held was blocked by a large post. "I don't want to miss any of Mike's match," I thought, so I decided, "I'll be extra careful while walking through the stands, and I'll be fine." When I stood up, a lady bumped into me, so I had to move quickly down the rows.

People could see me coming. Some even looked frightened— not for me—but for themselves. I could tell they were scared that I was going to fall and land on them. Everyone quickly moved over. When I finally made it to the main level—still intact, a few spectators even clapped.

I carefully started to walk over to the next section trying hard to be very "inconspicuous." When I reached the next section of bleachers, I did not see—because I was so pregnant I could not see my feet—a new mat adjoining the center mat I had just safely crossed. Of course, the mat was a bit higher than the floor, and, of course, I tripped.

At the moment when I tripped, another surprise greeted me— a man was right in front of me. As I began falling, I instinctively reached for something to stop my fall. I grabbed this man who had the misfortune of being "in my way"! I snagged his sweater at the collar and pulled it completely down to his waist. Disfiguring his sweater wasn't the worst of the situation. He lost his footing, fell down, and, of course, I landed right on top of him!

If only you could have seen the look on his face, my face, and my husband's face. But I guess the most surprised person was the man's wife who was walking in front of him. When she looked back, I'm sure the whole situation looked very questionable. Thankfully, she had a good sense of humor! When I apologized, we all began laughing. Probably the most amazing part of this entire story is that Mike was wrestling—oblivious to the sideshow I was providing for all the spectators!

I surely know how to create excitement during a mother-son double wrestling match. Oh, by the way, my son won, the man lived, and his wife "appeared" to accept my landing on top of her husband. I guess it truly was a victorious day!

Just a few hours later, I went into labor and delivered a beautiful, healthy, blue-eyed, baby boy who fortunately had no bumps on his head from the fall!

Teachings

1. Never stop cheering for your children through the wins and the losses in life.
2. Get involved in the lives of others no matter what consequences you face.
3. Leave your world and enter the world of others.
4. When you "trip up" in life, get up immediately and go on.
5. If and when you get embarrassed, learn to say sincerely, "I'm sorry," and laugh later.

―――

"My brethren, count it all joy when ye fall into divers temptations."
(James 1:2)

Meet More of My Family...

Our second son Mike; his wife, Ann Marie;
and their daughter Jada

Hey, Lady,
Thanks for the Gift!

One of the sweetest blessings happened to me on the morning of June 21, 2007, on my way to teach my summer school class at Hyles-Anderson College. I had decided that today was the day that I was going to use my coupon to buy a large cup of coffee for only 99¢ at my favorite coffee house, Dunkin' Donuts. Yippee!! "I get my favorite treat today!" I was thinking.

I often think that my car is remote controlled as it automatically drives me to the college when I leave my home. However, because it seems to drive on automatic pilot, I missed my exit to enter Dunkin' Donuts. "Oh, no!" I was already stopped at the light at the intersection of Route 30 and Route 41 before I realized that I had missed my turn. On that particular day Route 41 had been reduced to only one turning lane due to new construction. That made it even more difficult for me to reverse course for Dunkin' Donuts. After three attempts to turn at the light, I finally made it through the intersection.

"Oh, I'm not going to have time to get my drink at this speed," I thought. "Well, with only three extra minutes to spare, I'll drive through the drive-thru window."

Lo and behold, the employee at the window looked at me and acted very surprised to see me. "Hey, thanks for the gift!" she said as I stopped at the drive-thru window. I was a bit perplexed and

I'm wondering to what gift she was referring. She added, "Remember last week when you handed me that paper and asked me to take a few minutes to read it? Remember you said it could be the greatest gift I'd ever receive? Remember you said you couldn't do it for me, but you wish you could, and you'd like to see me in Heaven someday?" In her obvious excitement, she hardly stopped to take a breath before she began her next statement. "I did it! I did it! I trusted Jesus as my Saviour, and I will see you in Heaven. Thank you for sharing that gift with me. Do you have some more of those papers so I also can give that gift?"

I am without words to explain to you what this "stop" did for me. Yes, I have many, many blessings that take place in my life, but I also have a few blows. I promise you that in life the blessings way outshine the blows.

May we each realize the importance of asking the Lord every day to put the very people in our paths whom we might help, and then let's go help them. If we have trusted Jesus as our Saviour, we have a gift to give away that is for eternity. It is either Heaven or Hell. Who will be in Heaven because you or I cared?

I'll never forget the challenge that lady presented to me that day. I trust I will remember that statement, "Hey, lady, thanks for the gift." As I drove off, I started singing the following song:

Heaven is a wonderful place,
Filled with glory and grace.
I want to see my Saviour's face.
Heaven is a wonderful place.

But until then, my heart will go on singing.
Until then, with joy I'll carry on.
Until the day, my eyes behold the Saviour,
Until the day God calls me Home.

Will you share that gift with someone today?

Teachings

1. Pray daily for God to use you to be a witness for Him.
2. Carry tracts in your purse or in your pocket, and more importantly, share them on a daily basis.
3. Pray for souls and then go seek them.
4. Never, never quit. Get a partner and go soul winning every week.
5. Who will be in Heaven because you shared that "gift"?

———

"For the wages of sin is death; but the gift of God is eternal life through Jesus Christ our Lord." (Romans 6:23)

Meet More of My Family...

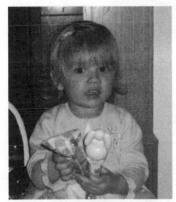

Above left: Jada Moffitt
Right: Jada and Ann Marie Moffitt

Meet More of My Family...

Right:
Joy and her buddy, her boxer Lexie

Below:
Joy's high school graduation with Mom and Dad

A joyful spirit keeps you young at heart.

Honey, How Long Have You Lived Here?

Several weeks ago our preacher challenged the folks of First Baptist Church to take one week and try to win as many people as possible to the Lord as a way to say thank you to the Lord for our 25,000 baptisms in 2006. Wow! What an exciting week!

I was so thrilled to actually get to go with my husband Roy and our daughter Joy to three different rest homes and assisted living areas on Wednesday, Thursday, and Friday of that week. It was so exciting to visit the many folks in the lobby, dining area, social center, and individual rooms.

Joy and her dad

When we started our services, my husband always introduced each of us individually, and we sang a few hymns. The people loved it. I remember on Thursday he announced, "And now for your personal enjoyment, we are honored to hear a special solo from my wife JoJo."

I almost swallowed my tongue whole because I don't sing! I used to sing solos in high school and even placed first in competition in Indianapolis at the high school state vocal competition. I also sang solos in the Catholic church from time to time. My special performance was in eighth grade when our class performed the operetta, *Bernadette*. Guess who was Bernadette? You got it right—me—even if I did give away the answer in an earlier chapter!

The first song performed in the operetta was the class singing in unison, and I was standing in front as they sang, "Bernadette so small and frail, she was weak and always so pale." The sight would have made anyone chuckle out loud as I am 5'10" in height, fairly strong, dark-skinned, and size 10 to 12. There was nothing small, frail, weak, or pale about me!

When I got involved in the bus ministry at our church, the singing resumed. Only this singing was hollering contests, seeing who could sing the loudest and smile. I always bought prizes for the winners. Every single Monday my voice was hoarse. I honestly believe that I would have contests on the bus so that I could win my own prizes. How crazy! After 42 years in the bus ministry, I know I have done damage to my vocal chords and can hardly sing today—but I still can yell the loudest on the bus when we chant, "We hate the Devil! We hate the Devil!"

So now, here I am at the rest home and about to make a singing comeback as I serenade my captive audience with the song, "Amazing Grace." Most of them appeared attentive, although as soon as I started, a few of them went to sleep. The one lady who seemed to take to me most said, "How beautiful!" I later found out that she wasn't wearing her hearing aids, and without them, she is practically deaf. She really was sweet and so kind. Before we left the room, she motioned for me to come over to her. She directed me to come down close to her face and said, "Maybe someday we can have lunch at my table in the dining room? Honey, how long have you lived here?"

"Oh no," I thought, "they actually think I'm one of the residents here!"

What a wonderful time we had with these precious folks. Over 22 people accepted Christ as their Saviour at the last service. One of these folks was that precious lady that spoke to me.

No, I don't live there, but someday we both will live together in Heaven because we both have put our faith and trust in Jesus Christ and accepted Him as our Saviour and only way to Heaven. Have you trusted Christ as your Saviour? I'd sure like to see you again.

Teachings

1. Love everyone that God puts into your path, and show your love through your smile, care, and tender words.
2. If you can't sing, do what I did. Fake it till you make it!
3. Realize there is no greater joy than to serve and meet the needs of others.
4. Get involved in some ministry in your church and give your heart to that ministry.
5. The rest home for many is their "last stop." Be "soul conscious" and try to win them to Christ before it is too late.

"They shall still bring forth fruit in old age; they shall be fat and flourishing." (Psalm 92:14)

'63 Homecoming Ends

Another homecoming has passed at WHS. JoJo Kinnane was elected homecoming queen to reign over the festivities.

The parade on September 19 brought honor to the seniors and juniors. The senior float took first place in floats and the junior car took first place in decorated cars.

Winner of the football raffled off by the Booster Club was Pam Geffert, junior.

Other senior candidates for queen were Etta Gima and Lorraine Serafin.

PICTURED LEFT: JoJo Kinnane, senior, is pictured being crowned homecoming queen by Don Justak, vice-president of the senior class.

One of my college classes at Hyles-Anderson College.

*People should feel better
when they cross your path.*

Meet a "Rare Bird"

I love to visit folks in the hospital, but personally, I don't ever like to be a patient myself. It seems like whenever I've had surgery, something has always gone wrong. You see, I'm truly a "rare bird," and I always seem to encounter weird complications.

One day I noticed a growth on my back and realized it was quite enlarged. When my husband noticed it and said, "What is that on your back?" I proceeded to say, "Oh, it's really nothing, nothing at all. It's a "slight" tumor, and when it bothers me, I'll have it taken off." Shortly after that, we scheduled a doctor's appointment only to find out it would have to be surgically removed.

I tried hard to convince myself and others that it would be fine without surgery and even just possibly go away. But no, the tumor just continued to grow—so much so that my blouse or jacket could no longer camouflage it. We knew we needed to have it removed, so we scheduled outpatient surgery just a few days later.

On the day of surgery, the doctors said it would be a simple procedure, but oh, were they wrong. As they deadened the area and started working on the removal process, I immediately advised them I could actually feel the cuts of the scalpel. They discovered in surgery that the tumor was much deeper and larger than they expected. It was actually so large that it filled up an entire cup. As a matter of fact, it was quite gross!

The doctor felt after the completion of the surgery that I

would be fine, so they allowed me to go home. I felt "fair" throughout the evening; but around 4:00 a.m., I woke up to excruciating pain at the site of the surgery. I went to the medicine cabinet and took the prescribed pain medication, but nothing seemed to help. Within minutes I started feeling lightheaded, and then I started to hear loud motor sounds in my head. Within seconds I passed out. My husband Roy literally dragged me from the hallway and laid me down on the bed.

I came to and heard my husband talking to the 911 operator, requesting that an ambulance be sent to our home. I still remember saying, "Roy, I'm okay. Please don't call an ambulance." (Of course, I was thinking of the extra cost of having an ambulance sent to our home to transport me to the hospital.)

Roy said that when he came back up the stairs to check on me, I was white as a ghost and extremely weak. My husband called the doctor at 5:30 a.m. only to be told to come immediately to his office so he could check out the situation. We arrived at the office at 6:00 a.m., only to learn that I needed emergency surgery. Can you imagine having two surgeries in less than 17 hours?

We soon learned that blood had filled the area where the tumor had been removed and formed a large clot. So now, that clot had to be removed.

"Oh great!" I thought. "I get to be opened twice!"

I was lying wide awake on the table, and realized there was no nurse to assist in the operation. My husband was drafted as the doctor's assistant! It was a day of surgeries I promise you I will never forget.

To make a long story short, I now have a large, permanent gash on my back because of the doctor's having to perform the emergency procedure and reopening the wound a second time. I also have a second scar where a drainage tube was inserted so the same thing would not happen again.

A few weeks after the two surgeries, I needed to go to Carson's Department Store for a dress fitting, and, of course, the seamstress noticed the wound. "Oh, Honey, whatever happened to your back?"

I quickly answered her with a rather grim look on my face, "I was knifed!"

"Oh, Honey," she said, "God bless you."

"It was rough," I continued. "I was awake during the entire process!" After I truthfully explained the entire situation, the seamstress got quite tickled.

Can you imagine how one simple surgery could be so chaotic? The removal of that "fatty" tumor ended up leaving a memory in my mind I'll never forget, and probably neither will you.

Teachings

1. Realize we never forget the "tough times in life." Learn from the "tough times" and in turn help others.
2. Learn to turn around the heavy situations of life.
3. Thank God for every day you are alive.
4. Learn to trust God to meet your every need in sunshine and in rain.
5. Never assume any surgery is simple. Surgery is like life; there are often many complications.

———

"...I am filled with comfort, I am exceeding joyful
in all our tribulation." (II Corinthians 7:4)

Meet More of My Family...

Above: Roy and JoJo Moffitt with son Roy, Jr., and daughter Joy

Below left: My son Mike with his wife, Ann Marie Moffitt
Below right: My son Jason and his wife, Allison Moffitt

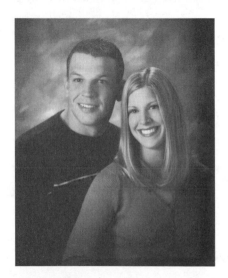 

Lift the spirits of others by showing joyful expressions on your face.

I Think I'm Losing It!

I think part of turning 60 years old is that I'm becoming a bit forgetful. The other day I hurried out of the house, got into the car, and had driven two blocks down the street when I realized I had forgotten something. I quickly turned the car around and headed back for home. I left the car running in the driveway and went into the house, ran up the stairs to get the....."Oh no, I can't remember what I forgot!" Until this moment, I still cannot remember what was so important to me that I went through all that rigmarole. One encouraging thing is that I now know I can hide my own Easter eggs, as I know I won't remember where I hid them.

Have you ever borrowed your husband's vehicle and driven somewhere, like to a shopping center? After you've completed your shopping, you return to where you thought you had parked your car, only to find it missing! You try so hard not to panic, especially when you realize he has a new car, you borrowed it, and now it's gone! In order to get the full picture, you must realize the new car belongs to both of us, but he drives it normally. I have an SUV that I love—it serves as my mini-office, containing paperclips, stapler, tape, folders, CDs, writing pads, cell phone and holder, hair spray, etc.

I tried so hard to retrace my steps—"Let's see, I came down row two, turned left...." Before I knew it, sweat beads were pouring down my forehead, and my heart seemed to be beating 150 times per minute. So I consciously slowed down my breathing and took slow and deep breaths. All the while I was doing this, I was walking through the parking area trying so hard to find my lost car.

Finally, as a last resort, I saw the mall security car and waved him down. "Sir, I can't locate my car. Would you please help me?" With his partner in the front seat, they let me sit in the back seat. He drove me up and down the rows, trying so hard to find my car. "We could call the Highland Police and file a report," one of them offered.

"Oh boy," I thought, "I can't be so forgetful that I have to have the police called. "Oh no, I sure hope the car has not been stolen!"

As we drove around the entire lot, we went down the last row. I glanced to my left and noticed a car that resembled my car that I thought I had left at home. I said out loud, "That's funny; someone owns a car like mine, same color, same broken window wiper blade."

As I continued looking at the car, the realization came that it was mine! "Oh no, that car over there is my car!"

Boy, did I feel foolish as I realized that all the time I had been searching for my husband's car, I had not even driven his car to the mall. I had driven my SUV there.

I'm so glad I didn't call my husband, Ron, I mean, Ray, no, I mean Rob? I know I'm getting closer…oh yes, it's Roy. Surely, I can't call "What's his name" to tell him my dilemma as he will surely think I'm losing it.

As you can see, it doesn't take much for me to have a good time. The funniest thing to me about this story is that I decided to share this story with my husband right after I wrote it. He got quite tickled, and then he decided to "confess" to me that he had had a similar experience recently in a Menard's parking lot. He also had a security guard trying to help him find his car, but he thought it had been stolen and did call the Hammond Police, only to realize he was driving my SUV!

As you can see, Roy and I truly are meant for each other. We both have so much fun in life and with each other as we relive all the unique and humorous experiences that come our way.

Teachings

1. Learn to laugh at the ups and downs of life.
2. Be good to your local police as you never know when you will need them.
3. Study your husband's picture carefully and practice saying his name over and over again so you won't forget him. (HA! HA!)
4. Wear your name tag if necessary.
5. Use your remote-controlled emergency button on your key ring to help you find your misplaced vehicle when necessary.

"Brethren, I count not myself to have apprehended: but this one thing I do, forgetting those things which are behind, and reaching forth unto those things which are before, Nevertheless, whereto we have already attained, let us walk by the same rule, let us mind the same thing."
(Philippians 3:13, 16)

Our Cinderella, Joy, and
Her Prince Charming, Todd Vaprezsan

Meet the Real Cinderella

I absolutely love the story of Cinderella. She was a beautiful scullery maid who loved to serve and in turn caused her evil stepsisters to become insanely jealous of her. She continued to live her life, no matter how they treated her, with kindness and care toward them and others.

I especially enjoy the night of the ball. When she realized it was almost midnight and needed to flee quickly home, she rushed down the stairs and actually stepped out of her glass slipper and continued on to the coach with her slipper left behind.

Well, it wasn't a glass slipper in my case, but a nice new pair of shoes that gave me unbelievable grief just a few years ago. My husband and I started a bus route to the Great Lakes Naval Base in Waukegan, Illinois, in order to bring the sailors to the Sunday services at our church. We actually drove 72 miles every Saturday morning and spent several hours visiting and encouraging the sailors to ride our bus on Sunday morning. We made the trip four times each weekend—to and from the base on Saturday and to and from the base on Sunday. It truly was one of the highlights of our lives to work at the base.

The sailors enjoyed the very exciting program on the bus for them, along with fresh donuts and milk every Sunday morning. After they attended Sunday school and the morning church service, we would load the bus and head for lunch at Kentucky Fried Chicken.

Right after lunch, we had a very exciting football game—

North against South. I can't explain the excitement we felt the entire weekend as we were able and privileged to minister to these young people. After the football game, they would load the bus again, and off to the Moffitts' house we would go.

I always fixed a home-cooked meal for everyone—including anywhere from 20 to 72 sailors each week. I loved fixing lasagna, spaghetti, tacos, or mostaccioli, along with salad, various desserts, and cold drinks. We became the sailors' "family away from home."

During our yearly Pastors' School, Brother Hyles asked us to bring a bus load of our sailors to sing the Navy song. You can't imagine how excited all of us were to be a part of this event. I went out shopping the week before and purchased a new red, white, and blue outfit, along with a new pair of navy heels. I wanted so much to look patriotic like "our" sailors.

The night of the event, the atmosphere was so thrilling. We all practiced our song and finally felt "ready" to go on stage at the Hammond Civic Center. Just as we were lining up, the tragedy of tragedies occurred. My three-inch heel broke off of my shoe. I didn't have a spare, so I felt totally at a loss. "Oh, no," I thought, "what possibly can I do to solve this dilemma?" I wanted so much to be a part of the program; yet, there was no way I could walk up the stairs and across the stage with over 5,000 people staring at me.

Quickly, behind the stage, the 45 sailors and with my husband tried to find a "twin Cinderella" with a pair of shoes I could wear. You won't believe it, but another lady behind the scenes wore a similar size, and her shoes were also navy blue. I felt so blessed and relieved.

Well, they were almost my size 10—they were an 8½ . I smashed my size 10 feet in the size 8½ shoes and happily participated in pain. The next week I made my way back to the shoe store, and the manager, after hearing my heart-wrenching story, replaced my broken shoes and even let me choose another pair as a bonus along with a sincere apology.

Yes, I believe this was my true Cinderella story and also a true test from the Lord. He took care of me and even rewarded me doubly.

Teachings

1. No matter what happens in your life, never give up and never quit.
2. Learn from Cinderella's strengths, and make them a part of your life.
3. Realize the blessing it is to serve in a ministry. What ministry are you a part of in your church?
4. Be a servant and enjoy it. Will you pattern your life after the traits of Cinderella or her stepsisters?
5. Never expect anything from those you serve. We went to be a blessing, yet we received a blessing that night as our church honored us by presenting us with a new freezer full of meat from a local butcher. This was a great blessing and help as we prepared our weekend meals in the future.

"Look not every man on his own things, but every man also on the things of others." (Philippians 2:4)

Meet More of My Family...

Above: "Nana" with two of my precious grandchildren,
Jada (left) and Aidan (right)

Above: Some precious photos of Aidan Moffitt
Below: Some precious photos of Jada Moffitt

*A grateful heart is a heart
full of joy, love, and compassion.*

By the Way, Have You Seen the Latest Pictures of My Grandchildren?

I used to think it must be pretty special for folks to have grandchildren, but did they have to seem so crazy about them? I now am a grandma, or "Nana" as my two younger grandchildren call me. Let me tell you— there is no way you can talk about them enough in this life. **THEY ARE ABSOLUTELY PRICELESS!**

We have five—Brooke is 17; Brandon is 16; Bryce is 10; Jada is 2½; and Aidan is 1. At age 60 I never thought a person could feel such joy as my husband and I are now experiencing. We can't wait for them to come over and hate for them to leave. I must admit though, I now know why God doesn't allow me at 60 years old to have a newborn child as my own. Whoa! I wear out after a few hours for sure.

Two Christmases ago I received $100 as a gift and decided to go shopping the week after Christmas at an outlet mall in Gurnee, Illinois. I knew I needed a few items, so I couldn't wait to shop. Just Joy and I! Yippee! We drove one and a half hours to the mall, ate lunch, and off we went shopping. The only handicap was me. I had just had my leg surgery, so poor little Joy had to push me in a wheelchair all day long. I loved it, but she really tired out by the end of the day.

The first store we visited was Value City. Oh my, the bargains! I found a sweater, two blouses, and a shirt—all for $98. I realized I would actually have enough change to buy a delicious cup of coffee at my favorite place, Dunkin' Donuts. As I sat in my wheelchair, I noticed a sign, "TOYS!"

I thought, "Before I purchase the clothing, I'd like just to glance at a few of their toys." Wow! What bargains I found!

I found a Clifford the Dog table and chair set, a toy box, and a ride-on toy all for under $100. I thought, "There is no room in our family room for these items, unless...yes, I'll remove my bone-colored leather chair and ottoman and form the new and exciting "Moffitt's Kids' Corner." That's it! So we purchased all the items for our "kids' corner" and put back all my clothes. Who needs clothes when you can have a "kids' corner"? (Well, please remember you do need clothes, just not new clothes—at least, not right now!)

I couldn't wait to get back that evening to redecorate our family room. Joy and I stopped for a late dinner at Olive Garden (another favorite place of mine), and then we drove home. We were tired, but it was a good tired when we got back home. Joy and her daddy helped unload the car and set up for our precious grandchildren.

Oh, I wish you could see it now. We have the same table and chair set, the ride-on toy, and "packed" toy box, along with a rocking horse, a buggy, a child's grocery cart, a large punching bag, games galore, tons of books, Play Dough, dolls, trucks, dishes, etc. Hey, after all, there is never too much for our grandchildren!

As soon as Jada arrives, she heads for the corner. She absolutely loves to play there and "share" with her younger cousin, Aidan. (Well, kind of share, they both are still adjusting to sharing all the toys.)

We have a trampoline outside, a pool, and even a brand-new swing set with three regular swings, a baby swing, monkey bars, a slide, and a glider. I decided to have a garage sale each year with my sister Cindy, and as always, I use the money for something special. Guess what I used the garage sale money for this year? Yes, you're right—a new beautiful swing set. You see, nothing is too good for our grandchildren.

I found a few sayings I'd like to share with you:

- "When you become a grandparent, you really do feel grand!"
- "Another miracle of life occurs when your child's child is born."
- "Grandparents are as cozy as a second comforter. They add an extra layer of love."
- "When you baby-sit your grandchildren, bring along your running shoes and vitamins."
- "You don't think you could possibly love your grandchildren more than you do today, and then tomorrow comes."
- "You can't spoil a grandchild with love."
- "It's important that your grandchildren know how precious their parents are to you."
- "A smile is the only way a baby can say, 'I love you.'"
- "Even before their grandchild is born, grandparents show off their first photo—a sonogram."
- "Grandchildren bring sunshine on a cloudy day."
- "The fear of flying can be overcome when there's a grandchild who lives 3,000 miles away."
- "When you count your grandchildren, you definitely count your blessings."
- "Having grandchildren doubles the pleasure of having children."

Some statements that need to be said to your children as well as to your grandchildren:
- "I love you."
- "I understand."
- "I'll always be here for you!"

––––

The time you spend with your grandchildren today gives them memories that will live on forever. Yes, I love every part of life as a "Nana" or a grandma. I realize I only have a few years to love, encourage, and influence their lives. As you can see, I'm quite engrossed in my newer title in life. Yes, if you see me, I have a "brag book"; and I don't mind showing it to you if you ask. Next time I see you, you just might want to be prepared. "By the way, have you seen the latest pictures of my grandchildren?" I'll be glad to show them to you.

Teachings
1. Children and grandchildren are a treasure that can't be measured in dollars and cents.
2. Grandchildren are the fountain of youth and make you feel so much younger in their presence.
3. Make your home, Grandma and Grandpa, a "home away from home."
4. No matter how many grandchildren you have, each one has a special place in your heart.
5. When you get together with your grandchildren, have lots of fun. You don't have to "act your age." You can act their age and get away with it—you're Grandma and Grandpa.

––––

"Lo, children [and grandchildren] are an heritage of the LORD: and the fruit of the womb is his reward." (Psalm 127:3)

You Don't Look Like a Preacher's Wife!

Several days ago I went to our local hospital with my husband to have some tests run. Amazingly enough, this time it was not for me but for my husband. We had found out a few days earlier that he had a ruptured disc in his neck that was causing him quite a bit of pain and discomfort. (No, I did not say I was the pain in his neck!)

How he injured his neck was quite interesting. He decided he was going to build a huge doghouse to house our 150-pound Rottweiler. Off he went to make preparations to build his master-piece. He decided to do this architectural design part in our garage and then move it out to the backyard after its completion. The house was so large, I could have lived in it or even used it as a guesthouse!

Never did he realize how large and heavy it would be to move it. Four men were needed to transfer it to the backyard. They first needed to lift it over a six-foot fence, but as they lifted it shoulder high, they lost their balance, and the house landed on my husband's neck. Oh, what horrible pain he experienced! I could see the excruciating pain written all over his face. The accident caused a ruptured disc and a spur on the vertebrae.

Now we needed to go to the hospital to check for nerve damage. Though surgery was ruled out, further tests were necessary. As we entered the testing area, a young lady needed to enter several bits of information into the computer. "Sir, what do you do for a living?"

He replied, "I'm a preacher!"

"Oh, I thought so," she immediately stated. "You look like a preacher."

Roy then asked, "And what does a preacher look like?"

She spoke right up, "He would be fresh in appearance, clean cut, and very friendly."

How true that is. My husband always looks sharp, very well-groomed, and "Officer Friendly" should be his name.

As she continued on to gather more information, I just knew I had to ask this important question: "Do I look like a preacher's wife?"

Immediately she said, "No!"

"What do you mean 'no'?" I quickly asked. I wondered why she didn't feel that I fit the bill of a preacher's wife. Did she think I looked like a floozy? (Whatever a floozy is!)

She appeared tickled as she answered, "Oh, I just picture a preacher's wife to be drab, dull, and in dark clothes. You are the opposite of that, for sure."

No, I didn't have on a pumpkin-orange dress with blinking lights on it, but she enjoyed seeing a preacher's wife in tasteful, attractive clothes and a smile to match—at least that is how she described my appearance.

I learned something that day that I never want to forget. People judge by the outer appearance more than we realize. No matter what life brings into our paths, may we never let it affect our outer spirit. Smile, cheer people on, look sharp, and be friend-ly. People need to see Jesus in you and in me, even through the storms and tests in life.

Teachings

1. Realize people notice your outer appearance first.
2. Next time you choose a dog, choose a toy poodle and put him in a decorated box. That way you'll avoid any type of possible injury. (In case you, too, try to build a doghouse.)
3. Be a "cheerleader and supporter" to your husband when he needs an encourager, especially during test times.
4. Look your best at all times, especially for the benefit of your husband.
5. Be proud to be a preacher's wife. Constantly strive to improve your attitude and your appearance.

———

"...*for the* LORD *seeth not as man seeth; for man looketh on the outward appearance, but the* LORD *looketh on the heart.*" (I Samuel 16:7)

Meet More of My Family...

Above: Grandpa's Father's Day gift in 2006 from Jada Moffitt
Below: Our precious Aidan Moffitt taking a rest

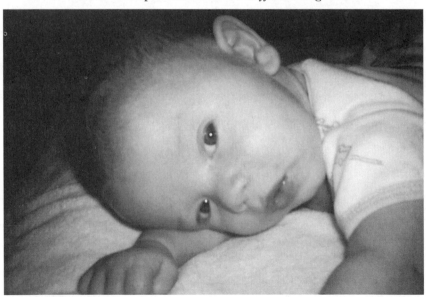

I'm Sleep Deprived!

I t's summer vacation, and I've decided that I'm going to treat myself to an on-purpose "sleep-in" until 7:00 a.m. Oh, what a wonderful idea! During the school days, our alarm clock goes off without fail every morning at 4:45 a.m. Can you see why a "treat time" of 7:00 a.m. would be so special to me?

The night before I laid out my game plan—hot shower, warm herb tea, and an extra remedy for great sleep, warm milk—YUCK—but it's supposed to help you sleep. I drank my heated glass of milk at 10:00 p.m. and another one for the extra boost at 11:15 p.m. I really wanted to sleep and be sure my night was truly restful.

At approximately 11:30 p.m., I headed for bed, but it seemed like two and a half hours before my brain shut down. I tried to count sheep, then cows, horses, ants, lice, etc.; but nothing seemed to work. I was wide awake for sure.

At 2:00 a.m., I glanced at the clock for the last time and finally fell fast asleep. Well, that was until around 2:30 a.m. when I was rudely awakened by the sound of sirens and fire trucks racing past the front of our house. As I heard the blaring sounds, I immediately prayed for God to protect the firemen and meet the needs of the person who had placed the emergency phone call.

It is now 3:00 a.m., and I am really tired. Off to dreamland I go, only to be interrupted around 3:30 a.m. by a loud crash that seemed to take place right underneath our bedroom in our garage. "Oh no, is someone trying to break into our home?" I thought I knew I needed to check out the situation, but I was almost too tired to care. I grabbed a fireplace shovel for protection and headed for the garage. As I attempted to push open the door, I felt great resistance against the door. My first thought was that someone was pushing against the door and holding it closed. I finally forced the door open just enough to see that a ladder had somehow fallen across the door, partially blocking it.

It is now 4:15 a.m., and I desperately need some rest. To sleep just an hour sounded so good, but I just couldn't get back to sleep. I tried to block my mind to all that had occurred and finally returned to "snoozeville."

Around 5:45 a.m., I was awakened for the third time to our three dogs' incessant barking. "Oh no, now the dogs are my challenge!"

Let me introduce you to Cain, Lexie, and Zander. Cain is a bull terrier that belongs to our son and is staying with me, "Grandogmother," until they get a home and out of their apartment. He is a stocky, overly active dog that looks like a cross between a horse and an anteater. If I am washing our patio door on the outside, he loves to run "playfully" as hard as he can and knock me down. He is so precious!?!

Our beautiful boxer, Lexie, is our priceless pet and the mother of our third dog, Zander—a very lively and large puppy who has the strong spirit of his daddy, Cain, and yet has the shy, sweet spirit of his mother, Lexie. The three dogs together create a bit of a zoo at our house, to say the least.

By now I am really awake due to the blessing of their incessant barking. After about five minutes, they finally stop barking; that is, two of them stopped. Zander refused. He would not hush.

All of the sudden, I remembered that my husband taught me a trick to get them to quiet down if necessary. All I needed to do was to throw out a glass of water at them, and they would stop.

"No problem, I can do this," I thought.

I opened the window and saw Zander barking up a storm. I immediately went to the sink, grabbed a glass, and filled it to the brim. I was so excited as I walked toward the window; all would soon become calm, peaceful, and serene.

Almost chuckling out loud, I aimed and threw the water to hit the dog smack in the face...or so I thought. Unfortunately, just as I threw the water, my husband walked out into the backyard to see what all the barking was about, and the cup full of water hit him instead of Zander! Was my husband drenched!

He was not laughing, but I was doing everything in my power to hold in the laughter. The dog did stop barking, but the look on my husband's face looked like a dog about to attack. He paused a few seconds and then got tickled.

I called from the second-floor window, "You're right, Honey; water does stop the dogs from barking."

Well, I guess I created another precious "JoJo Moffitt Moment." I believe the only time I will rest and have quiet time and peace will be in the casket. It seems that with the way I live, as soon as they close the coffin, the trumpet will probably sound, the Rapture will take place, and I'll need to get up again!

I'm so glad I'm alive today, and I pray that I will learn from every situation God puts into my path. I pray that in turn I might encourage and help others. How about you? What has God chosen for your path today?

Teachings

1. Take care of yourself, and try to get the necessary rest on a daily basis. (6 hours? 8 hours? 30 minutes? HA! HA!)
2. Learn to turn the heavy situations around and find the good in them.
3. Enjoy every step of life—sleep or no sleep.

4. Put a smile on your face and turn someone else's frown into a smile.
5. Thank God for your life and for giving you another day to live and give.

"Behold, I shew you a mystery; We shall not all sleep, but we shall all be changed." (I Corinthians 15:51)

*People are drawn to people
who possess joy.*

Don't Panic in an Elevator

Oh, how I detest elevators! There is a reason why, I promise. We were shopping one day at Water Tower Place in Chicago. I was pushing our one-year-old son, Justin, in a stroller, and our three-year-old son, Jason, was walking a bit ahead of me...right toward the elevator. Before I knew it, he walked very briskly and stepped into it before I could catch up. The door shut—he was inside, and I panicked! My mom and my sister, Cindy, were with me. One headed up the stairs, and the other went downstairs.

I pushed the button and tried my best to find my young son. Oh, I cannot explain the fear that was racing through me as I realized we were in downtown Chicago, and he was all alone with many people he had never before seen. Area news had just reported that a child had been kidnapped the week before in that general area, so you can imagine what was going through my mind.

*Roy with our youngest sons,
Justin and Jason Moffitt*

On the elevator, I pushed the button to go to the floor below, and to my amazement, when the door opened, my son was standing with a security guard, along with my sister who had found him. I definitely fear elevators!

The week our new auditorium opened for the first time, I had a similar incident take place, but this time it was I who felt lost, forsaken, and definitely all alone. As I entered the building and started toward the elevator, I noticed one of our church security guards. Being a little cocky and funny, I said, "If I get stuck in here, you won't leave me in here all alone will you?"

He laughed and said, "Yes, Mrs. Moffitt, we'll pretend we didn't even see you get in there, and in turn, leave you there." I continued on my way and entered the elevator. Before I knew it, the doors closed behind me.

All of the sudden, my mind started playing games with me. "What if I really did get stuck? No one was really in there with me, so no one would know I'm here all alone to rot and suffocate to death." My mind was going in many different directions but not the direction I wanted it to take.

It seemed like hours, but I know it was just a minute or two, and the elevator did not move. "Oh, this is horrible, and if I scream, the security guard will think I'm fooling around. Oh no, what will I do?" I truly broke into a sweat, and my heartbeat picked up and went full speed ahead. "Maybe I'll suffocate or have a sudden heart attack. How embarrassing to die this way!" I thought.

Needless to say, my emotions took over. In fact, they went way overboard. I started to talk to myself. "Okay, JoJo, calm down; everything is going to be okay. Surely there is enough air in here to last a little longer...at least, maybe five more minutes?"

As I took a few deep cleansing breaths to regain control of myself, I looked at the panel and realized I had never pushed the floor number. As a result, the elevator was standing still. I pushed the number 2 button and off we went. Was I ever excited to get out of that elevator and share my exciting story with the guard. How very glad I was to be in control and not panic in an elevator.

Learn from me—the next time you enter an elevator, don't panic; remember to push the button. If needed, use the emergency button and then scream as loudly as you can!!

Teachings
1. Be relaxed and in control—like me!
2. Pray—don't panic.
3. Don't be afraid, as help is literally just a step away (or at least we hope so!).
4. Laugh at your "boo-boos."
5. Be nice and not cocky to security guards. You may need their help someday.

"Trust in the LORD with all thine heart; and lean not unto thine own understanding. In all thy ways acknowledge him, and he shall direct thy paths." (Proverbs 3:5, 6)

Meet More of My Family...

*Above: "The Moffitt boys" at Mike and Ann Marie's wedding
(left to right) Jason; Roy, Sr.; Mike; Justin; and Roy, Jr.*

*Below left: Jason and Allison Moffitt
Below right: Justin and Emily Moffitt*

Learn to find joy in the little things of life.

"Please Let Me Drive the Electric Scooter!"

Arlys Cooper

I've always had a hidden desire to drive those electric scooters you see in grocery stores and places like Wal-Mart. My friend, Arlys Cooper, who also is a coworker at our college, has very crippling arthritis and has to use a scooter to get around. I can't tell you how many times I have teasingly threatened Arlys to take her scooter. She laughs every time I share my desire.

After I had an injury to my calf muscle many months ago, I truly was getting "stir crazy." I was laid up for nine weeks due to the injury and possible blood clots. One day my friend, Janet Moore, asked if she could do anything for me that I'd enjoy. I said, "I'd love to go for a ride in the car." She came by, and we loaded the wheelchair, crutches, and me into her van for our outing. I was so thrilled to get out again and hear the birds and see a lot of activity, flowers, and trees. It was great! After we took our short ride, she asked if I had any special place I'd like to go. Where do you think I wanted to go? You're right; one of my favorite places in the whole world to shop is Wal-Mart. So off we went to Wal-Mart.

As soon as we entered the store, I saw my hidden desire—the electric scooter. Yippee! I now had a legitimate reason to use one of these vehicles with my handicapped leg (and brain). The greeter tried to give me instructions regarding the use of the scooter, but I hardly heard her as I couldn't wait to start the ride. After the "training," I took off on my vehicle. It was so much fun! I did great until I was entering the office supply area. Janet asked if she could leave me for just a minute or two and go to the next aisle to look at greeting cards. "Go ahead, Janet. I'll be fine by myself."

As Janet walked away, I turned from the main aisle to go down the aisle where the office supplies were lined up. What I didn't know—because I had "missed" something during the earlier training time—was that when you turn into a smaller aisle, you need to make your turn wider. Because I didn't hear the instructions, I turned sharply, hit a large display case, and then watched several hundred pens, pencils, and school supplies go flying everywhere. I didn't know what to do except to keep going, as the employees readily assured me that they did not need my help. "We will clean up the disaster," I heard one of them say.

I was so shaken. I started to proceed forward but hit the wrong button. Now I was going backward. I ran the scooter over one of the employee's legs. Did I ever cause some chaos!

You know, I think now that I'm back on my feet, I'll just play it safe and walk everywhere from now on. May I let you in on a little secret—I still love motor scooters, but I'll play it safe and walk, not drive, from now on.

Teachings

1. Learn to enjoy the little things in life.
2. Learn to laugh when you "mess up."

3. Cherish your health while you have it.
4. Take scooter lessons before you drive. Think of all the injuries you could avoid.
5. I'm rejoicing that Wal-Mart still lets me shop there. (HA! HA!)

"Brethren, I count not myself to have apprehended: but this one thing I do, forgetting those things which are behind, and reaching forth unto those things which are before, I press toward the mark for the prize of the high calling of God in Christ Jesus." (Philippians 3:13-14)

Meet More of My Family...

Above: Justin and Emily Moffitt with two of the "grandogs," Toby and Chloe

Below left: Justin and Emily Moffitt's wedding
Below right: Justin and Emily Moffitt stop at Monticello while on tour for Hyles-Anderson College

*To help you through the pains of life,
learn to create joy daily.*

What's the Holdup?

During the Christian Womanhood Spectacular, our annual ladies' conference held at First Baptist Church of Hammond, a decision was made to have a Christian Womanhood mall with stores that would be open during the breaks for the ladies to shop. I was very honored to be asked to organize this area and found the opportunity to be very exciting and challenging.

On Monday, two days before the conference, I taught my classes at our college, went home to prepare dinner, and then went to the church to help with the setup for the mall. My daughter-in-law, Emily, had spent the earlier part of the day working with several of our students to help prepare the booth areas and decorations for the mall. By the time I arrived, she was "in the heat" of the work and doing an excellent job.

Soon after I arrived, she realized her car keys were missing. She went over to the area where she had left the keys, only to find they were gone. It appeared that someone had picked them up or thrown them away by mistake. Poor Emily.

We called the car dealership only to be told we would have to have the car towed in and a new key system made for the vehicle. What a disappointment this caused. In turn, I tried to find the cheapest generic towing company to help her. On the phone I was quoted one price, but by the time the truck arrived, the price had "magically" become higher. After several minutes of dickering on the price, the man loaded the car on a trailer and took it to the dealership...only to find out later that he had taken it to the wrong dealership! It was like a bad dream.

After we solved the "car mystery" and found the car, I decided I needed a little break and some relaxation. I decided to go to the grocery store and pick up a few groceries, along with some treats for the workers helping with the construction of the mall.

I literally walked ever so slowly toward the store, trying to relax by taking deep, cleansing breaths. Just as I entered the store, another customer came in at the same time and we were walking side-by-side. She appeared very upset and even confused. She looked me right in the eye with a hard stare and loudly stated, "I hate life! I hate life!"

I told her, "Life is great; it is what you make it!" She hurried past me, and as she walked toward the customer service area, she pulled out a gun.

"Oh, brother, so much for relaxation. I don't have to be concerned about completing this mall; I'm about to die!" The two ladies who appeared to be with her grabbed her arms and were quickly assisted by a store security guard.

You ask, "Was the gun real?"

I promise you that I did not say to her, "Excuse me, ma'am, may I check out that item you're holding? Is it real or not?" I found out later that it was a BB gun, and she had been in and out of mental institutions for several months.

Needless to say, I was very glad to get back to "normalcy" at church and forget about my relaxation idea. I promise you that God must love me specially to feel I need events like this to happen in my life—that's what the holdup was that night.

Has anything exciting happened to you lately?

Teachings

1. Enjoy and treasure each day of life.
2. Stay out of grocery stores (just kidding).
3. I judge my blessings by my blows—how about you? We had a very successful mall and a tremendous conference. It was life-changing!
4. Learn to turn the heavy situations around and find joy.
5. Don't ever quit when the trials come. I plan to do the same job at the conference this year. I can't wait!

———

"And the peace of God, which passeth all understanding, shall keep your hearts and minds through Christ Jesus." (Philippians 4:7)

Meet More of My Family...

Above: Roy's brother and sister-in-law, Denzil and Phyllis Moffitt

Below (left to right): Becky Griffith (Roy's niece), Charlotte Griffith (Roy's sister), Alex Denkowski (Roy's second cousin), Sue Denkowski (Roy's cousin), and Rachel Segura (Roy's niece)

Don't look for ways to find joy; look for ways to give away joy, and then you will find true joy.

The Day My World Literally Turned Upside Down

In April 2006 I had the tremendous privilege of speaking at the ladies' conference at the Bethel Baptist Church in Walls, Mississippi, pastored by our dear friend, Dr. Ron Westmoreland. He and his wife, Miss Kim, are wonderful friends to our family and ministry. It was a tremendous meeting, but, as always, after just 24 hours away, I was very eager to return home.

My husband always makes me feel special when he picks me up at the airport and often takes me on a date to a restaurant in Chicago for dinner on the way home. As my plane landed, I saw I had a message on my cell phone. I immediately played it back only to be very confused by the message. "Mom, this is Justin [our son]. I'm on my way to the airport to pick you up, but I am a little confused about which airport to come."

That message was not at all like our son. He is normally very organized and first class. I now was really confused as to why he didn't know where I was. I was also wondering, "Where is my husband Roy?"

I was finally able to talk to Justin personally, and he very calmly explained to me that while my husband was en route to the airport to pick me up, he was talking to Joy, our daughter, on the phone. A lady missed her exit off the Dan Ryan Expressway and turned directly in front of my husband's car going at least 55 miles per hour. In turn, it was impossible for my husband to avoid the accident. On impact my husband's car flipped over and landed upside down. God watched over my husband in such a great way. As the car flipped over and skidded upside down, the vehicle never exploded nor was it hit by other cars on the same highway.

My husband was literally hanging upside down by his seatbelt. He had to disengage the belt and then crawl through the driver's side window that had been blown out by the impact. He then was taken by an emergency trauma team to the Northwestern Hospital trauma unit in downtown Chicago. All this time, we never knew his condition.

Meanwhile as I was still speaking to Justin, I felt "frozen" at the airport as he directed me to take a taxi from the airport to meet him and his wife Emily at the hospital. I truly felt numb, but Justin walked me through every step on what to do and where to go.

I got my bag from the baggage claim area and headed for a taxi cab. As soon as I entered the cab, I asked the driver, "Could you quickly get me to Northwestern Hospital? My husband has been in a bad accident."

The cab driver proceeded to say, "Was the accident on the Dan Ryan Expressway?"

I said, "Yes!"

And he said, "It's on the news right now. They have the jaws of life on the way, and it is not known whether or not the person involved is a fatality."

I thought, "Oh my, surely Roy will be okay. Please take care of him, Lord, and protect him right now."

As we started our drive, it hit me; surely there is a reason for this accident and a reason why I'm in this cab right now. I shared this thought with the cab driver, and it seemed to tenderly touch his heart. He then started crying while he was driving, and he shared his heart with me.

"I killed my wife last week," he choked out.

I thought, "I think I'm having a bad dream. Right now, I don't know if my husband is alive or dead, and this man is now confessing to me that he murdered his wife." A few minutes later I realized that he had confused his wording. He felt his wife had died because he gave her the normal dosage of her daily medications, and one of them had caused her to bleed to death.

Within minutes I assured him that he did what he was supposed to do in being so diligent to care for her needs, especially with her medication schedule, but that God chose the day his wife would die, and he had had nothing to do with her actual death.

He thanked me over and over again, and I truly felt that God had allowed this emergency to happen so this cab driver could be helped. As we pulled up to the emergency room entrance, Justin came out to meet me and to help me with my luggage. Justin looked a bit confused when he saw that the taxi driver was sobbing. "Mom, what has happened to this man?"

I answered, "I got to help him tonight." Justin looked very confused and perplexed. To see the man sobbing, it did indeed look like I had somehow broken the man's heart, but he said I helped him, right?

I was so relieved to be at the hospital and to walk into the trauma unit and see my husband talking and alert. He actually was having an "upbeat" time as he relived the last hour and all that had taken place.

After the paramedics placed him in the ambulance, they went back to his car and found a large box of makeup in his backseat. They had so much fun with that box. "Sir, may we ask you a question?" They showed him the large box of makeup and asked, "Could you explain what this was doing in your backseat?" My husband laughed and assured them that the box belonged to his wife—that's me.

As soon as I arrived at the hospital, believe it or not, the same paramedics arrived again with another patient. They wanted to meet me and get an explanation of "the goods." I had no idea what had happened when they asked me about the makeup. We looked down, and to our surprise, someone had placed that box of makeup under his gurney! (It just kept following him.) I quickly picked up on what had been happening and said, "I don't know why he insists on wearing makeup; it's really embarrassing to me." Without a doubt, we all had a very hearty laugh over that makeup box.

A lady in the next cubicle came out and said, "I've never ever seen people have such a good time as you folks are having tonight—especially in a trauma unit."

Dr. Tom Vogel, the academic vice-president of Hyles-Anderson College, who is my boss, and his son Jimmy came all the way from Indiana to Chicago to visit my husband. When he could see Roy was doing so well, he teased him and said, "I thought you were critical. If I had known you were doing so well, I wouldn't have come." They all laughed and yet rejoiced that he was doing so well.

Later that evening the doctors decided to release Roy from the hospital—no broken bones and a slight minor cut on his forehead, but alive and just quite shaken up.

Before we left, we knew we needed to talk to the lady in the next cubicle. Since my husband is clergy, he went to visit her and encourage her. Within minutes she had sweetly trusted Christ and told my husband that she felt he had had the accident and been taken to Northwestern just for her to ask Jesus to be her Saviour.

What an exciting day this had been! As we started for home, we all realized that none of us had eaten, so off we went to one of our favorite restaurants, Cracker Barrel. My husband treated, especially since we didn't have a car (ours was totaled), and he wanted to say thanks to Justin and Emily for being there and helping us through the whole ordeal.

At the restaurant it was so special as we met several folks from our church. Roy shared his "story of the day," and all were glad that he was okay. When we finished our meal, I handed Justin a $50 bill and asked him to please go pay the bill for us. The total bill was $42.98, and we left a $7.00 tip.

As were were walking out of the restaurant, one of the employees called my name. "Mrs. Moffitt, did you already pay your bill?"

I thought, "Oh no, she thinks I'm walking out without paying, and I had Justin pay it for me." I just happened to have the receipt in my hand and quickly showed it to her.

She said, "Oh no, I don't need to see your receipt; it's just that someone left you a gift at the register." She then handed me a $50 bill with a note that said, "A love gift for the Moffitts." What a wonderful surprise! Right at that moment, my daughter-in-law Emily started crying. She then said, "I wondered at the hospital who was going to send food to us as you and your husband are always taking food and treats to people when they have a need like this. Instead God wanted us to go to one of our favorite restaurants, Cracker Barrel, and choose a hot meal, and He paid for it!"

Yes, definitely, my life was turned upside down and then back again. How I thank God for His protection, love, and special care—especially the treat at the end of the day at Cracker Barrel. How perfect!

Teachings

1. Realize we make mistakes, but God never makes mistakes.
2. Be soul conscious of everyone who crosses your path.

3. Love your husband before he's taken from you.
4. Turn the heavy situations in life around, and don't live "down."
5. Praise God in the good times and the bad.

"In every thing give thanks: for this is the will of God in Christ Jesus concerning you." (I Thessalonians 5:18)

Justin and Emily Moffitt (Christmas 2006)

*Learn to develop
an attitude of joy and gratitude.*

Meet the Yoga Man

It's summertime, and I just know today is the day I'll finally get to walk at our town park and achieve two to three miles of good exercise. I tried to do it two days ago and made it around four times only to regress and make it all the way around only one time yesterday. Was I ever disappointed.

You see, two years ago I was playing a simple "kids' game," and in the process of completing the game and possibly winning or losing by one point, I ripped my right calf muscle right from the bone. Are you wondering whether or not we won? Yes, we did; we won by one point, but I, in turn, did major damage to my leg. I probably need to be planning games for our sweet rest home folks instead of nearly killing myself at age 59 playing a simple kids' game.

As I started my walk, I had hardly made it one fourth of the way around the track when my hips and knees started burning unbelievably. "Oh, this is not good," I thought. I'm sure I must have showed my discomfort on my face as an older gentleman who was running the track graciously stopped to help me. I soon learned he was from Iran, had a PhD, and worked for a petroleum company. He gave me some great instructions on how to slow my pace, relax as I walked, and even instructed me about food. "No meat," he said. "Stay away from animals, just fresh fruit and vegetables."

He even went further to sit on the grass and try to show me how to do yoga to reduce stress and to relax. Can you just see me sitting on the grass doing yoga and seeing my husband drive by? I know he'd think, "This time she has really flipped!"

The man continued, "Did you know that you smile a lot and speak to everyone?" It's amazing how people watch you (even when you're in pain). He opened the door for me to witness to him when he asked me, "What makes you so different?"

I proceeded to tell him that I had prayed this morning for the Lord to allow the very people into my path that I might help today. So I surely did not want to miss the opportunity to speak to my new friend, the "Yoga Man" (that's what I called him). It was so sweet, as within minutes, I was able to share how my life has been changed since I trusted Jesus Christ as my Saviour, and in turn, I was able to lead him to Christ right there on the track at the park.

By the way, do you know 100% for sure you're on your way to Heaven? It's a gift from God for you and for me. What do you have to lose, but better yet, what do you have to gain? You have nothing to lose, but everything to gain.

You can know. I John 5:13 says, "*These things have I written unto you that believe on the name of the Son of God; that ye may know that ye have eternal life, and that ye may believe on the name of the Son of God.*" The following is what you need to know to be saved.

1. WE ARE ALL SINNERS.
    Who is good? Romans 3:10, "*As it is written, There is none righteous, no, not one.*"
    Who has sinned? Romans 3:23, "*For all have sinned, and come short of the glory of God.*"

2. WHERE SIN CAME FROM
    Romans 5:12, "*Wherefore, as by one man sin entered into the world, and death by sin; and so death passed upon all men, for that all have sinned.*" ("One man" is the first man, Adam.)
    Revelation 20:14, "*And death and hell were cast into the lake*

of fire. This is the second death." The words *second death* in this verse mean Hell.

3. GOD'S PRICE ON SIN
   Romans 6:23, "*For the wages of sin is death; but the gift of God is eternal life through Jesus Christ our Lord.*"
4. OUR WAY OUT
   Romans 5:8, "*But God commendeth his love toward us, in that, while we were yet sinners, Christ died for us.*"
   Romans 10:13, "*For whosoever shall call upon the name of the Lord shall be saved.*"
   Romans 10:9-11, "*That if thou shalt confess with thy mouth the Lord Jesus, and shalt believe in thine heart that God hath raised him from the dead, thou shalt be saved. For with the heart man believeth unto righteousness; and with the mouth confession is made unto salvation. For the scripture saith, Whosoever believeth on him shall not be ashamed.*"
5. YOU MUST ASK IN FAITH.
   Hebrews 11:6, "*But without faith it is impossible to please him: for he that cometh to God must believe that he is, and that he is a rewarder of them that diligently seek him.*"

Ask Jesus to save you now. "Dear Jesus, I know that I am a sinner; if I died now in my sin, I would go to Hell. Right now, by faith, I am trusting You as my personal Saviour and my only hope for Heaven. Thank You for dying on the cross for me and for saving me from an eternity in Hell. In Jesus' name, Amen."

If you did say this prayer and really meant it, God says you can be 100 percent sure that you will go to Heaven. Please let me know if you made this decision by sending a note to JoJo Moffitt, 1016 Fran Lin Parkway, Munster, Indiana 46321. I would love to hear from you.

Meet More of My Friends...

David and Trina Reynolds and family

Children standing left to right:
Brittany, Jaclyn, and Amber Dawn
Seated: David Jack

*'What you think on is what you are—
thankful, happy, joyous, and loving
or angry, fearful, bitter, and negative.*

Watch Your Mouth!

James 3:10 is a very powerful and soul-searching verse of Scripture to live by and to challenge us every day. *"Out of the same mouth proceedeth blessing and cursing. My brethren, these things ought not so to be."* Words are a means of expressing what is in our minds and hearts. What did you express today, and how did you express it?

Proverbs 8:6-8 says, *"Hear; for I will speak of excellent things; and the opening of my lips shall be right things. For my mouth shall speak truth; and wickedness is an abomination to my lips. All the words of my mouth are in righteousness; there is nothing froward or perverse in them."*

I still remember my dad's famous words to me while I was growing up when I often expressed exactly what I thought! "JoJo, think before you speak!" and "If you don't have anything nice to say, then don't say anything at all!"

"That's okay," I thought. "I just won't talk anymore." Needless to say, that didn't work either.

I truly try hard to use words to express friendship and love to my loved ones, friends, and folks that cross my path. Sometimes expressing my friendship and love is through a smile, an encouraging word, or just a simple wave of the hand.

One of my favorite families is David and Trina Reynolds and their children, Jaclyn, Brittany, Amber Dawn, and David. Trina was married to her first husband, Steven Staton, for four and a half years, only to discover he had cancer, and he died 33 days later. He left a beautiful 23-year-old widow and two daughters who were two years old and five months old. Five years later God gave her a new husband, David Reynolds, who is a gem!

While Trina was a widow, we enjoyed "spoiling" her girls with treats, picnic lunches, shopping at the Dollar Store, and special phone calls back and forth. (One time when I was ill, they called to sing to me, and I replayed that message over and over again until it was erased by mistake when our phone broke.)

One of my favorite treats is to look for the girls when I find my seat in church and show my love by blowing a kiss to them along with a friendly wave. One particular church service, I spotted them and immediately sent off my usual greeting with a wave and blowing a kiss. I didn't believe they saw me the first time, so I did it again. Oh yes, they saw me and responded, but the man in front of them, who happened to be a visitor, saw me at the same time. He looked at me and then looked all around to be sure I was trying to "get his attention."

"Oh my, what have I done?" I thought.

He immediately smiled, looked right at me, waved, and blew a big kiss directly toward me. I'm sure he felt this was a very, very friendly church because of my overly "friendly" behavior. Needless to say, I'm now very careful when I send such greetings!

Many months ago I was facing some pretty "good" challenges regarding my health. I already have incurable kidney disease in both kidneys, and at this writing, my liver enzymes are quite elevated. When you have a mom who died with pancreatic cancer and a sister who also died of cancer, red flags go up. As I was preparing to go to Mayo Clinic in January, some words were sent my way that were quite encouraging.

First, the week before we left, my husband, my daughter Joy, and I visited the Build-A-Bear store in our local mall. I couldn't believe that store and all you went through to choose and "bring to life" your personal bear. I loved looking at all the outfits, the accessories, the birth certificates, the stuffing of the bear, and especially all that went into choosing a heart, warming it, and placing it inside the bear before he was stuffed. I was so consumed with the process that I actually started crying when the bear was completed. My husband and daughter had to comfort me in my tears and literally escort me out of the store. I'm sure my motherly behavior was really a bit embarrassing for them. It must have looked like I had just said goodbye to my soldier son being shipped overseas, and all my heartbreak involved was a bear being stuffed. Needless to say, I've never had a bear—much less a special bear from a place like Build-A-Bear.

The night before I left for Mayo Clinic, my daughter Joy, and her boyfriend Todd surprised me by making me a beautiful brown Build-A-Bear named Hope Joy dressed in a red-and-white party dress, red-and-white hair bows, white ruffled socks, and ruby-red glittered shoes. The best part was that Joy and Todd each placed a message inside the bear to love and encourage me while I was gone from my family and possibly facing major surgery. (Surgically, I'm classified very high risk, so it was an extra concern to my children at that time).

My daughter Joy with Todd Vaprezsan

The message from Joy said, "Mom, Todd and I wanted to get you something special as you go away on your trip to Mayo, so we decided to get you Hope. We hope you enjoy her. We love you lots and lots, and we'll be praying for you. See you soon."

The message from Todd said, "Mrs. Moffitt, I just want you to know that I'm praying for you while you're away. If you ever feel lonely, scared, need a friend, or just need a hug, feel free to squeeze Hope's hand just to remind you how much Joy and I love you."

What a precious, priceless "gift of words" this bear was and has been to me. Yes, I did take Hope Joy with me and squeezed her hands often. It worried my husband a bit as I teased him by saying I was taking Hope Joy EVERYWHERE I WENT AT MAYO CLINIC!

Can you imagine what each of us could do to "pump new life" into family and friends by the way we choose to give encouraging and uplifting words?

I also received a letter from Joy that she wrote the night before I left at 12:20 in the morning, and she left it under our bedroom door. May I share with you a "prize letter" that was written to build her mom and put a new fight for life in her and to encourage her to never give up and quit!

Dear Mom,

I just wanted to write you a note and tell you that I am thinking about you and really have been praying for you! I am gonna miss you a lot while you are gone at Mayo. I want you to know you'll greatly be missed! You haven't left yet, and I already can't wait for you to get back! The reason I am glad you're going is so that they can find out whatever is the matter with you and then fix it! I hope no surgery has to happen, but if it does, I know it'll be for the best.

Please don't ever feel like you should ever give up! You still have an 18-year-old daughter who has a lot to learn about life and...marriage, and needs someone to cry to when I have a problem whether in a relationship or at college! And an 18-year-old who needs her only mother to help her through all that! I need you to help me with my homework and term papers, push me to do more for my bus kids, encourage me to love more people through your teachings, and most of all, I need your love!

You're the only one in the world that can give me the love you have given me. Mom, you can't let me down. You need to keep on keeping on. I love you so much and the deepest way I can love, I truly do love you! I need you for a long time. I am practically only a child. I am only getting out of one stage of my life…and now it's time for me to face the real world—college, teachers, dating seriously, marriage, my future ministries. And the only person I know that can teach me the best is my mother.

If you feel not needed, just stop for a second…and realize I'm still a child that is just learning to stand—not yet ready to take my first steps into the world, but I need that little push, and no one else can push me better than my mother. Who else is going to be there for me to help me along the way?

You and Dad have done such a great job to finally get me out of my baby years and finally stand and go to college, but I still have a long way to go before I am finished. So until then (which will be never), I'll need you. And if you ever feel like giving up and you're not needed at the college, first realize that you have a daughter who wants you there and needs you there, but you are also there to make a big difference in tons more girls' hearts! I love you so much, and I don't know if this note totally makes sense, but it's truthfully from my heart. I need you.

Love ya,
Joy

——

My daughter, Joy, and her boyfriend, Todd Vaprezsan, were a "B-12 shot" and a booster shot to me at a very tender time in my life. I love to live, and I promise I will not quit! Much thanks to Joy and Todd.

Teachings

1. Give your life away to others and encourage people in as many ways as possible.
2. Watch what you say and how you say it.
3. Pray for ways to encourage people and then go put it in action.
4. Who is going through a rough time? Why not go and choose a talking Build-A-Bear for them?
5. Be careful to whom you blow kisses. You also could get yourself in a very embarrassing situation.

"Let nothing be done through strife or vainglory; but in lowliness of mind let each esteem other better than themselves." (Philippians 2:3)

Joy and I at Justin and Emily Moffitt's wedding

A life of joy creates positive feelings.

I Made a Real Hit in Louisiana

Someone recently asked me if I have any unique memories from any of my travels (not that I travel that much), but I definitely have some. I especially remember when I traveled to Baton Rouge to be part of a lady's conference at Central Baptist Church pastored by Dr. B. G. Buchanan. I had only been in Louisiana one time, so this trip was a special treat for me. Mrs. Marlene Evans and Mrs. Carol Tudor conducted the early sessions of the conference, and I remained back at the college to teach a Friday class for Mrs. Evans. Then off I went to join them.

When I arrived, it was time for me to be introduced as the next speaker. I came in and sat in the back as Carol completed her session. As I was being introduced, I began making my grand entry from the back of the church to the front. I wanted to relate with the

My boss, friend, and mentor,
Marlene Evans

ladies right away as I'm a born and bred Yankee. I always say, "I'm a Yankee with a Southern heart!" To me, Southern people always seem so sweet.

I shared how I was intrigued with alligators, and that on my first trip to Louisiana, I got about five feet away from a six-foot alligator in a pond. I explained that I honestly didn't realize how dangerous alligators can be, and I actually tried to feed this one raw chicken. Of course, I had to illustrate how I tried to feed that "pet." Holding my cordless microphone in one hand and my notes in the other, I began acting out how I tried to coax the alligator to come to me.

Envision me stooped over the alligator's pond trying my best to call the alligator to come to me. "Come here, Mr. Alligator, come here!" As I was illustrating my moving toward this critter, I did not realize I was on a raised platform. When I was introduced, I remember noticing that the platform did not have a center microphone and that the main podium instead was on the right side at the front of the auditorium. What I did not know and for some reason had still not realized was that the platform was elevated about eight to ten inches above the floor.

Before I knew what had happened, I lost my footing and landed flat on my face. I just knew I had broken my foot; I could even feel it beginning to swell. I thought, "How can I ever get out of this?" Still holding my notes and my microphone, I started laughing.

Mrs. Evans was seated on the front row, and she started laughing hysterically. Now everyone in the audience is joining in as I am flat on my face in mortal pain but determined to get back up. I tried so hard to get up all the while acting like I wasn't in pain. I finally hobbled to a raised chair that had been placed on the platform, all the while feeling my ankle swelling and throbbing unbelievably.

The man who was videoing the conference was quite mystified. "Here I am taping JoJo, and all of a sudden, she disappeared. She was gone! I couldn't find her until I saw her start crawling up on her knees, attempting to reach that chair!" It's amazing all that can happen to me when I leave town to visit some wonderful Southern friends for just a few hours.

The following Tuesday I was scheduled for a checkup at Mayo Clinic for my kidney disease. While there, I just happened to mention my right foot. The x-ray found not one but three bones were chipped in my right foot! Have you ever noticed I always seem to be in the midst of some kind of excitement? I promise you I don't look for excitement. It always seems to find me!

Teachings

1. Learn to laugh at yourself when you "mess up."
2. Capture memories wherever you go.
3. Try to put a smile on someone's face.
4. Relive the fun memories of your past.
5. Get up and go when you get hit with disappointments in life.

"Make me to hear joy and gladness; that the bones which thou hast broken may rejoice." (Psalm 51:8)

Joy Moffitt
today

Marlene Evans planned a shower for Joy Marlene. My daughter Joy
is the namesake of Joy Evans Ryder and Marlene Evans, of course.
Mrs. Evans is holding a picture of her daughter Joy (then).

Are You Going the Right Way?

I've never received a ticket from a police officer in my life. As I write that statement, I'm truly not being cocky—just rejoicing! Notice I didn't say I've never been stopped. I still remember one time as if it were today. I had just gone by to visit my mom in my hometown of Whiting, Indiana. After leaving my mom's home, I got into a traffic jam. Since I knew the area so well, I decided to take a quick turn down an alley and take a side street to the main road.

I turned from the alley onto this street, and within one minute, I saw this unbecoming light flashing on the top of the car that was following me. I felt led to pull over. Very confused, I got out of my car and walked back to the police car, still wondering what kind of help I could be to this man.

The first words out of his mouth appeared very stern. "You're going the wrong way, lady!"

As I looked into his car, directly next to him on the seat were several Gospel tracts. You see, that particular week we were having Pastors' School at our church with a soul-winning theme for the entire conference. Each day my pastor had asked me to share for ten minutes with the entire congregation a soul-winning experience that I had had. The only words I could think to say to the policeman were, "No sir, I'm going the right way. How about you?"

I knew I was on my way to Heaven, and within minutes, I was able to share with that concerned Hammond policeman how he also could know. After a few minutes, right there in his car, he bowed his head and trusted Jesus Christ as his only way to Heaven. He thanked me so much, and I went on my way. He was so grateful; yet, he was so consumed with what had just happened that he never explained why he had stopped me.

"I wonder why he stopped me?" I was puzzled as I continued to drive down the street. I knew I wasn't speeding. I knew I had used my turning signal to signal my intention. I was wearing my seatbelt. Suddenly I noticed all the parked cars were facing in the opposite direction of the way I was going! After driving several blocks, I finally spotted that one-way sign the city had hidden from me! Can you believe that my hometown made a perfectly good two-way street to a one-way street without consulting me?!?! (HA!)

The next day as I was on my way to Pastors' School, I stopped for a light near our church. I looked to my left, and believe it or not, in a car right next to me was that same policeman. He looked at me, smiled, and pointed to Heaven. I couldn't resist. I said to him, "Yes, there's only one way." I then pointed to Heaven and said, "Now we're both going the right way."

Teachings

1. Be soul conscious at all times.
2. Faithfully pass out Gospel tracts.
3. You can turn a wrong into a right.
4. Set a goal to witness on a weekly, or better yet, a daily basis.
5. Point others to Heaven.

"For God so loved the world, that he gave his only begotten Son, that whosoever believeth in him should not perish, but have everlasting life." (John 3:16)

Magnificent
Moffitt Moments

This summer has been extra special, especially during the times we were to spend with our children and grandchildren. Father's Day was extra special for sure. All of our married children who live in the area came over for our Italian pizza party with Italian bread, my husband's favorite pizza, antipasto salad, and delicious chocolate whipped cream cake. Yummy!

Mike, Ann Marie, and Jada Moffitt

Our son Mike and his wife Ann Marie have been blessed with one daughter, beautiful 2½-year-old Jada. They went through a real heartbreak this past winter when they lost a baby in a miscarriage. We are rejoicing as they recently found out that Ann Marie is expecting a baby, due to be born around December 10, 2007. We are so thrilled for them (and for us, too). Our son Jason and his wife Allison have a one-year-old son, Aidan, who is a real doll. He is so funny and full of life. My how we love them. Our son Justin and his wife Emily have each other, and they have two precious dogs, Chloe and Toby.

I thought it was quite unique and special, as on this Father's

Allison, Aidan, and Jason Moffitt

Day, Chloe gave birth at 3:15 p.m. and 4:45 p.m. to two adorable puppies, her first litter. Justin and Emily were traveling with the Joyful Melodies tour group from Hyles-Anderson College for three weeks as the tour preacher and wife. Since they were gone, I was the dog sitter and midwife to the mom dog. The whole family witnessed the entire labor and delivery of the pups. I thought it was really special that the pups were born on Father's Day. We can now say, "Happy Father's Day, Justin!" I became a granddog-mother. Pretty unique, huh?

At the end of June, we decided to take a different kind of vacation. We have been privileged to have our daughter Joy travel and sing for Hyles-Anderson College for eight weeks this summer. She has had a dream since the seventh grade to make a tour group, and her dream came true this summer 2007.

The second part of the blessing was to find out that our son Justin was going to be the tour preacher for the first three weeks of the summer with Joy's group, the Joyful Melodies. We decided to drive 15 hours to hear Joy sing and Justin preach. (We took an extra three hours due to a mess up in roads.)

*Justin and Emily Moffitt (left) and Roy and JoJo Moffitt (right)
with the Hyles-Anderson College tour group, the Joyful Melodies,
Sarah Delgado, Laura Taylor, Kim Butler, Joy Moffitt,
and Joy Kerns, (left to right)*

We were so thrilled to hear Justin preach three nights and to hear the girls—Sarah Delgado, Kim Butler, Laura Taylor, Joy Kerns, and Joy Moffitt—sing so beautifully each night. I can't explain the tears of joy I shed as I watched my children serving the Lord.

We decided in the four days we were there that we would be a part of the preaching services, and then on the fourth day, treat the girls to a "fun day." And a "fun day" it was, as they all were able to go white-water rafting for a couple of hours. Everything went smoothly until the last half hour. I was actually taking pictures as their boat came over a bank, and out flew my daughter Joy, my daughter-in-law Emily, and Sarah Delgado. They all got soaked and shaken up and yet were thrilled beyond measure.

I never felt so helpless to see them in that condition, and I couldn't do anything to help. My husband tried to reassure them before the adventure how safe and secure they would be. I'm sure it is a memory they will remember as long as they live. (I'm just glad they lived!)

The tour group had many memories on tour, but one special one was at the mall one day. They noticed three men from UPS all glancing at them, as all five girls dress alike everywhere they go. The girls in turn walked up and greeted them cordially. They mentioned that since the men were all dressed alike, and the girls were, too, maybe they could get a picture together. After they snapped a couple of pictures, the girls were able to share where they were from and how they were on tour this summer. Within minutes they shared their testimonies and were able to lead all three men to a saving knowledge of Christ. What an exciting trip to the mall!

Yes, these are just a few memories of summer, but oh, what priceless memories. Being privileged to be married to Roy Moffitt and to be the mother of six and grandmother of five so far, I am able to capture priceless memories every day of my life. How about you?

P.S. Just as I completed this chapter, I noticed the mother boxer, Chloe, seemed quite agitated in her cage with her puppies. I couldn't imagine what was bothering her and why her puppies were whining. Did I get tickled when I realized it wasn't Chloe, our son's dog, in the cage. It was our boxer Lexie. I had put her in the cage accidentally, and she was trying to nurse the puppies. Oh well, another "Magnificent Moffitt Moment" for sure!

Teachings
1. Be a cheerleader for all your children in the wins and losses of life.

2. Capture memories in your mind and heart.
3. Relive the memories and learn to laugh.
4. Realize with family, you haven't helped them until you've first been inconvenienced, but when you love them, you never know you've been inconvenienced.
5. If you have a boring life, pray for your own "Moffitt Moments."

———

"Not that I speak in respect of want: for I have learned in whatsoever state I am, therewith to be content." (Philippians 4:11)

The Joyful Melodies and their tour preacher, Justin Moffitt, and his wife, Emily

Meet More of My Friends...

Above: The Hyles-Anderson College summer tour group,
The Joyful Melodies, Joy Moffitt, Sarah Delgado, Laura Taylor, Joy
Kerns, and Kim Butler (left to right)

Below: The Joyful Melodies and Emily Moffitt dine with Mrs. Renee
Cox and Mrs. Shelly Youmans, Liberty Baptist Church, Durham,
North Carolina, at the English Tea Room.

Sir, Can You Please Help Me Get My Husband Ready for His Autopsy Today?

Have you ever thought through something you were about to say so carefully and then you still messed up? Well, I did it, and I did it royally! Last Wednesday my husband was scheduled for several biopsies, and to say the least, my mind was consumed with the procedure.

I tried so hard to stay active and busy as I helped him care for many necessities that needed to be done in case he was out of commission for a few days. For a few moments I caught myself dwelling on the negatives. "Lord, I really don't want to be alone while he is in surgery. I just don't want to be alone."

My husband was "honored" with a sixtieth birthday party!

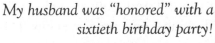

Within seconds it was as if the Lord put His arms around me, and a sense of comfort totally surrounded me. I realized that He never ever leaves me, and He would be with me better than anyone else could. I just knew everything was going to be fine.

Can you imagine how ridiculous I felt when I called the doctor's office the day of surgery (trying so hard to appear caring, calm, and in control) and asked for some needed advice. When the receptionist answered the phone, I immediately asked if I could speak to the doctor's nurse. "Sir, my husband, Roy Moffitt, is scheduled for an autopsy today at 1:15 in the afternoon, and I just wanted to know if he could take a couple of Tylenol to relieve possible discomfort and pain? You see, I want him so much to be comfortable."

The receptionist said, "An autopsy? We usually don't do autopsies here. They are normally done after death at the hospital."

"Oh no, I can't believe I actually said he was having an autopsy!" I felt so foolish as I realized that not many "loving, caring wives" would care so much that they'd "plan" their husband's autopsy and even go to the extent to make sure the procedure was comfortable for him.

I hoped so much they would forget my "boo-boo" by the time we arrived. At 1:00 p.m. we arrived at the office and walked up directly to the check-in counter. "Roy Moffitt has an appointment at 1:15 p.m. with the doctor."

As soon as I said, "Roy Moffitt," all four employees looked directly my way. They then asked us to have a seat, and they'd be with us shortly. As soon as we walked off, I could hear them chattering and whispering. I turned around and walked back to the window and chimed, "Are you having a fun time over my 'goof up'?"

They said, "Honestly, it's not normal to have patients call

preparing for their loved one's autopsies!" We all had a good, hearty laugh over my antics.

Hey, what did they expect? I'm definitely not normal; to me, normal is boring. Anything happen to you lately in your life that is exciting and "normal"?

Teachings

1. Go above the "call of duty" to help your loved ones.
2. Think before you speak. Okay, so you did think and this happened anyway. Just learn to laugh, really laugh at yourself.
3. Try to turn all negatives into positives. It sure helps keep your spirit up.
4. Realize God is in control and with you even in the tough tests in life.
5. Next time you plan an autopsy, do it anonymously. That way you won't feel so stupid when you get caught.

"...I am filled with comfort, I am exceeding joyful in all our tribulation." (II Corinthians 7:4)

Meet More of My Family...

Above: Roy's sixtieth birthday party given by the Ladies' Outreach Soul-Winning group from First Baptist Church of Hammond, Indiana

"Papa" Roy and Jada Moffitt

Never take for granted the joy of living.

A Fourth I'll Never Forget

I truly love America, and I especially enjoy all the festivities that take place to celebrate the birthday of our great country on July 4. This Fourth of July is one **I'll never forget**! Our son Jason was enjoying the fireworks, only to have one backfire on him and cause second-degree and even third-degree burns to his hand and thigh area. He ended up spending time in the local emergency room and had to see a plastic surgeon. It is so difficult to see your own children (ours are all grown now) suffer; Jason is facing a very painful recovery and possibly even plastic surgery.

Two of our married sons, Mike and Jason, spent the Fourth of July with their wives' families; so our sons, Roy, Jr.; Justin; Justin's wife Emily; my husband and I made the very best of the Fourth—"this five were quite alive!" We went to my hometown of Whiting, Indiana, to watch the yearly Fourth of July parade, along with my sister Cindy, her husband Tim (who had open heart surgery March 2007 and is recovering well), and their twin daughters, Katie and Karen. We had a great morning spending some time together.

When we arrived back home around 1:40 p.m., we found a message on our answering machine we were expecting. However, it was not necessarily one we were overly eager to receive. The previous week my husband had a biopsy, and we were told we'd receive the results in about seven days. They also said that since the seventh day was July 4, not to expect hearing from the office until July 5.

But the message stated, "Mr. Moffitt, this is Dr. Unni, and I'm calling about your biopsy results. We found some areas of concern that we would like to discuss with you face to face. We would also like to schedule an appointment to discuss your options." I knew this was not a positive report, so I called Dr. Unni. At that time the doctor explained to my husband in detail what the biopsies had revealed. About 1:50 p.m. we learned that the biopsies showed my husband has prostate cancer!

I honestly felt like I was frozen for a few minutes. "Could this possibly be a bad dream?" I thought. "I'll surely wake up in just a few minutes." No, it was a new mountain to climb when you've been chosen for the valley. Right then I began to sing, "God is so good. God is so good. God is so good. He's so good to Roy and me. He answers prayer. He answers prayer. He answers prayer. He's so good to Roy and me."

I know we are sold out for the Lord and plan to serve Him until we die. My prayer is that He will use this and every part of this condition to bring Him honor and glory. I know He loves us and trusts us so much to allow this new challenge into our lives and the lives of our family.

Right after the call, my husband said, "Hey, there's another parade in Munster [the town in which we reside] at 2:00 p.m. Let's go and keep our minds busy." So off we went to parade number two for the day. You have to understand that parades are endured by my family—I love parades, but they graciously endure only one a year. I was thrilled as now I got to be a part of two parades! Yippee!

As we were walking near the parade site, I saw a police officer from our town whom I thought I knew. I said, "Are you Officer Stribiak?"

He stated, "No, but I know you. You're JoJo!"

I thought, "Oh, no, how does he know me, and do I want to

know how he knows me?" This is not the time to ask how he knows me!

I'm notorious for saying "cute" statements. For instance, I remember the day I met a lady for the first time who said to me, "Do I know you?"

I thought about it and jokingly said, "Sure, remember I was in the cell next to you at the Lake County Jail." Why I said that, I'll never know, but I really said it.

She immediately said, "You're kidding! I just got out!"

Oh, did I have some explaining to do to her. Afterward, we both laughed when I attempted to clear up that situation of my own making.

We didn't linger to hear how this particular officer knew me! Instead, my family continued walking to the parade route. As we walked, I made a comment right as the parade began. "I'd love to have an American flag." Can you believe it? A lady came by minutes later, out of nowhere, and gave each of us an American flag. Isn't God good how He answers even our desires?

The temperature started to rise near 90°. What do you think was the next statement to come out of my mouth? "Oh, if only I had some water!" I had hardly mentioned the water when a man walked by in the parade and handed me and each of my family members an ice cold bottle of water. Please remember we had just learned about 40 minutes before that my husband has cancer. I honestly felt like the Lord was reaching down personally to love and encourage our family. Yes, God is always so good.

Lastly, as the parade was about to conclude, a float came by with several elderly folks about 75 to 80 years old riding on it, representing a high school 50+ class reunion. Their class mascot was a tiger, so the former Hammond Tech Tigers were on a float that resembled a huge cage, and they were the tigers inside. The leader of the group had a loud, powerful megaphone, and he was chanting old cheers. Within seconds I heard him say, "Hey, lady! You with the striped red, white, and blue shirt!"

"Oh no," I thought, "I'm not about to look down! I did wear a striped shirt today!"

He proceeded to say, "Hey, remember me, your old boyfriend? Remember when you dumped me for that younger guy next to you? I bet you're sorry now. You could have been in the parade with me today had you not dumped me!"

I felt like I was redder than the brightest red apple you could imagine. I have never so much wished I could disappear. By this time everyone around was laughing hilariously—especially out of control were my children and the man I dumped him for, my husband. (By the way, I never saw that man in my life—I promise!)

I thought again, "Oh how much the Lord loves us and encourages us through humor." Yes, you can have even more joy through the ups and downs of life. I plan to have joy; how about you?

Teachings

1. Realize God is always good no matter what He allows into your path.
2. If you ever feel down, quickly turn it around.
3. You can be positive or negative; the choice is yours. The positive sign is a + or a cross. The negative is a – or a half cross. I beg you to take up your cross (+) and follow Him.
4. Learn from what the Lord allows into your path. Don't miss what you are supposed to learn. I would hate to go through the "teaching times" and miss the teaching. Remember, often you can't really care until you've first been there. We're there and plan to care.
5. Life is a parade. No matter what happens, keep marching. I challenged my daughter Joy who was on tour for Hyles-

Anderson College when we heard the news that her daddy has cancer, "Joy, this is a part of life. We're sold out to serve the Lord, and we will always keep marching forward because we're the 'Marching Moffitts.'"

6. Remember that God is good.
   "God is so good.
   God is so good.
   God is so good.
   He's so good to you and me."

"...I am filled with comfort, I am exceeding joyful in all our tribulation." (II Corinthians 7:4)

The Moffitt family in Hawaii, May 2005

Meet More of My Family...

Above: Roy, Jr.; Justin; Joy; Mike; and Jason
Below: Roy, Jr.; and Joy Moffitt

I Think I'm Cracking Up

"**I** think I'm cracking up." You are probably getting a bit tickled at this comment as you say, "I thought you cracked up a long time ago, JoJo Moffitt." Sometimes I think we put ourselves in such stupors over the things that happen to us that we literally think on things long enough that we almost feel like we're going through the situation.

Brother Hyles used to say, "Most women have either just cracked up, are in the process of cracking up, or will crack up in the future as soon as time allows." Let's not be the one who plans on having a "breakdown," that is, as soon as we have enough time to plan one.

To be honest, I feel so much that this "down thinking" is caused when we think and think and think on negatives until we feel like we are absolutely going "bananas."

Brother Hyles taught us that when people have voids in their lives, they actually feel like they are losing their minds. They need to fill the empty spot and not let the negative thinking creep in. He said that depression is caused by a vacuum. We need to keep the voids filled so depression cannot get in.

I just decided a long time ago that I'm not going to let my mind control me, but I'm going to control what I think and what passes through my mind. You can also control your mind. Realize that no matter what you are going through today, God allowed it, and He will help you get through it.

The greatest counselor is the Lord. Don't let life's situations build up to the point where you just feel like you are going to explode. Go to Him with the problem, especially when it occurs, and say, "Lord, You know what is happening, and I beg You to give me the grace and the wisdom to know how to handle it." Don't dwell on it. Put it in His hands and don't take it back. Let Him help in making your decisions.

I just love I Thessalonians 5:18, which says, *"In every thing give thanks: for this is the will of God in Christ Jesus concerning you."* This verse has been a great help to me. Yes, JoJo, when your son has to go through surgery again, give thanks. *"In every thing give thanks...."* Our son, Roy, has had a total of 18 surgeries, one after another. Several were reconstructive surgeries from a congenital thyroid and ligament disease. Roy has been a real trooper—what an example he has been through his radiant smile and his joy. He truly shows his Christlikeness, I believe, through his face, his spirit, and his attitude. What an example he is to me!

I have had to consciously think to myself, "That wasn't a mistake, JoJo. The Lord says, 'In every thing give thanks: for this is the will of God in Christ Jesus concerning you.'"

What's happening in your life right now that you think is causing you a hard time? May I say that the Lord says, *"In every thing give thanks...."* Yes, there will be rough, hard times, but please know that the Lord is in control. Don't dwell on it and worry; but instead, think on it, pray, beg God for wisdom. Beg God to take care of this situation and pray, pray, pray. Just keep on praying till light breaks through. Just keep on praying; God is going to take care of you. He will take care of me, too.

Yes, there will be tears and concern, but oh, what victories! Each time we left Roy, Jr., at the entry to the operating room, I felt like Abraham offering up his son Isaac. When the nurses escorted Roy through the doors that led to the operating room, I honestly felt like I had put him on the slab—I just didn't have the knife in my hand, as Abraham did, but the doctors did. I watched and waved as they left us and as Roy smiled at me and said, "I love you, Mama. If I don't see you here, I'll see you there," and pointed to Heaven.

Every surgery Roy went through taught me to care more and more for others, especially the families in the surgery waiting room. We used that time to serve coffee, donuts, soul win, and encourage others. As I have already mentioned, the Christian life is like a cross and the plus or positive sign in math (+). I know I am not always a positive thinker, but I try. I believe it is good and healthy to be a positive thinker. Did you ever think about it? A cross is a positive sign; a minus sign is a "take away" or negative sign. Don't be a minus sign or half-rate. Be a positive (+) Christian.

When you are going through the hard times, do you ever consider I Corinthians 10:13? *"There hath no temptation taken you but such as is common to man...."* In other words, other people have faced problems, and we are going to face them. Also, if you think about it, most people have it a lot worse than you and I do. *"...but God is faithful, who will not suffer you to be tempted above that ye are able; but will with the temptation also make a way to escape, that ye may be able to bear it."*

What!! That's what the verse says. He will not let anything happen to you more than you can take. *"...but will with the temptation [trial] also make a way to escape, that ye may be able to bear it."* He is not going to let anything happen to you that you can't take.

Remember, when you are going through the hard times, don't give up. Don't even think about it. Go to someone who cares— the Lord, your preacher—and let them help encourage and guide you. Go to them and have them pray with you.

I would like to share another special verse. Nehemiah 8:10,

"...the joy of the LORD is your strength." When you have been hit and weakened, the Lord says that the joy of the Lord will be your strength and your armor. You know when you've met a "down person"; that person shows it with his facial expressions and negative spirit. Please don't be a "downer." Be an "upper" to all who meet you. Always remember that through the weak times, God is right there with you. He is putting you through some trials and tests to make you a better Christian and to make you a stronger person in general.

Did you know that you're going to help people more by facing the actual problems and going through them rather than by just reading about them? If you have gone through a trial or faced a test, you are going to know a little bit more how the person feels as you have also experienced that same trial. The person who has lost a child more easily understands the heartbreak of another who has experienced the same loss. I lost two babies—one in 1980 and one in 1986, and I believe I can easily empathize with those who have lost children.

No, I'm not cracking up! I plan to live my life trusting the Lord and serving others. How about you?

20 Ways to Keep From Cracking Up

1. Wake up daily and rejoice in the Lord that you're alive.
2. Read your Bible on a daily basis, sing, and pray for others.
3. Keep your voice tones and attitude upbeat.
4. Kiss your hubby and kids when you first greet them and when they leave.
5. Enjoy what you do, and show it on your face and in your attitude.
6. Don't complain, but instead, think on the good and tell it to others.

7. Keep yourself neat and sharp in your appearance.
8. Keep your home in good, clean order.
9. Do something for someone else on a daily basis.
10. Be faithful to all church services.
11. Get in a ministry and enjoy it.
12. Have a Bible verse as your daily verse, and recite it over and over again.
13. Use replacement thinking when you think negatively.
14. Smile. It shows warmth and encouragement.
15. Set goals for the day.
16. Be thankful and play "show and tell." Show people you love them by telling them personally how much you love and appreciate them and then tell it to others also.
17. Count your blessings; name them one by one, and go be a blessing to others.
18. Live by a schedule.
19. Be an encouragement to all you meet.
20. Take every opportunity to witness to others and share how they, too, can know for sure they are on their way to Heaven. Be soul conscious to all you meet, everywhere you go.

———

"I can do all things through Christ which strengtheneth me."
(Philippians 4:13)

Roy, Jr. and Todd Vaprezsan at Disney World

Joy and Roy, Jr.
at Jason and Allison
Moffitt's wedding

The Blessing of Bus Kids

Today is Sunday, June 24, 2007, and I'm really excited to be able to ride our Sunday school bus another Sunday. I have been privileged to be in the bus ministry at First Baptist Church of Hammond, Indiana, for the past 42 years. I have been the bus captain of Route 32 for 37 of those 42 years. I truly love our bus route.

Today seemed a little different and more challenging as I prepared for the day. I woke up very early and yet after having a good night's sleep, I was extremely fatigued. I felt like I was "dragging" in every attempt to get ready. Within a matter of minutes, I realized the reason for this fatigue. I discovered I was bleeding internally from my kidney disease called medullary sponge kidneys. I was diagnosed at Mayo Clinic in 1970 and have been battling with it since that time. I really have done quite well with it; in fact, I have done better than the doctors ever expected regarding the progression of the disease. It is a disease that normally affects one kidney, but I always do things special, so I have it in both.

With medullary sponge kidney disease, the kidneys actually calcify as the result of hundreds of stones that cause multiple infections and internal bleeding. The natural progression can, of course, impair the kidneys and their function. The specialists say I now have over 100 stones in both kidneys. When one of those stones decides to move, it is like shards of glass cutting flesh, and that cutting causes the bleeding. The resulting blood loss can be very draining and even tougher when the infections occur.

When this occurs, I immediately start taking Cipro, a medicine for this condition, and start pumping the water through my system. One thing I do every Sunday is early "phone wakeup calls," and even with my flare up, today is no different. Maybe I can't go to the homes and pick up the riders, but I can make the calls and be on the bus to love and greet each rider as they step inside.

My first call was quite interesting. "Hi, this is Mrs. Moffitt from First Baptist Church and Bus 32, and I'm calling to wake up the children today." Immediately, the lady on the phone replies, "What? I don't have any children. I have two sick dogs, and I don't like you or your church."

Oh boy, did I ever make a mistake! In error I had dialed one wrong number in my attempt to wake up and encourage our riders.

I waited a moment and decided to call her back. She actually answered and spoke before I could utter a word. "I told you I don't have any kids, and I don't like your Baptist church!"

"Ma'am, I'm truly sorry, and I apologize for calling you in error," I quickly stated and very humbly apologized. "I was reared as a Roman Catholic all my early years, and now for the last 42 years, I have been a highly involved Baptist, loving and working with people about whom most individuals don't care. We love bringing them each Sunday, and I just try to help them by calling them to get them up to get ready. I'm so sorry I upset you. I really am. It has nothing to do with our church. It has to do with me; I just dialed wrong. Please, won't you forgive me?"

She quickly said, "Uh, oh sure."

I truly felt so bad, as I'm sure she was broken. Maybe a sick dog or two had kept her up all night. Remember, don't retaliate; just humbly apologize.

It was so precious when each of the riders hurried to the bus full of excitement. One of our riders is four-year-old Reuben Mercado. Both he and his mom are so faithful and ride every week. Reuben is like sunshine every time we see him. As he entered the bus, a big smile broke across his face, "I love you, Mrs. Moffitt!" His mom, Nancy, always dresses him like a sharp, neat "little man." We had only been on the route a few minutes, and as we made a stop, Reuben hollered, "Mrs. Moffitt, I have to tell you something."

Since we were stopped, I motioned him to come forward to my seat. He looked me right in the eyes and said, "Mrs. Moffitt, you are a 'bootiful' lady!" A little while later, it happened again.

Nancy and Reuben Mercado
Bus Route 32

"Mrs. Moffitt," he yelled, "You're cute!" After he told me three times I was "bootiful" and two times I was cute, the other riders started saying, "You're a good mom, Mrs. Moffitt. You're our best friend, Mrs. Moffitt." It's amazing how contagious good words are just as negative words can do damage.

Again, I learned so much from my precious bus route. I'm so glad I didn't let the fatigue of the beginning of the day keep me from enjoying and learning from the bus kids. What a blessing they are to my life!

Roy and JoJo on
Bus Route 32 (1977)

Teachings

1. Be consistent in whatever ministry you are a part of in your church.
2. Think on the good and tell it to others.
3. Be a blessing, not a cursing, to everyone who crosses your path.
4. Don't let disease keep you from serving God.
5. Love your bus riders and tell them often of their good traits. Don't just correct them all the time. There is power in praise.

———

"Out of the same mouth proceedeth blessing and cursing. My brethren, these things ought not so to be." (James 3:10)

———

P.S. If you have read my first two books, you read about our bus rider, Wilbur Hoover. He is 52 years old, educable slow, and *still* plans to marry me after my husband dies. It's nice to know someone is waiting for me, isn't it? Wilbur always wants to share blessings and encouraging words. My how I learn from these precious folks.

The workers of bus route 32 (Missing is Joy Moffitt who was on tour for college.)

Let joy always remain in you.

You Are My Sunshine or Are You?

Yes, we each can be sunshine in a very cloudy world. Did you ever realize how important words are, but more important is how we express them? Words are a means of expressing what is contained in our hearts. What did you express today to the folks who crossed your path?

"Hear; for I will speak of excellent things; and the opening of my lips shall be right things. For my mouth shall speak truth; and wickedness is an abomination to my lips. All the words of my mouth are in righteousness; there is nothing froward or perverse in them." (Proverbs 8:6-8)

Be kind.

"She openeth her mouth with wisdom and in her tongue is the law of kindness." (Proverbs 31:26)

Talk kindly no matter what people say or do to you. Recently, I met a lady who I had not seen in several years. Her first words were, "Your coloring looks bad. Are you okay? It's really good to see you because I heard you had died."

Do you think those words were really encouraging to me? Yes, I obviously am alive and really doing quite well. When people ask me, "How do you feel?" I always say, "Great! I am doing great!" Yes, I know I have a kidney disease and multiple health problems, but I "do my best and hang the rest." I often say, "Fake it till you

— *251* —

make it." Yes, I have health concerns, but they don't control me or my spirit. I fake it till I make it, and I've made it great so far.

Smile.
"Rejoice in the Lord alway: and again I say, Rejoice." (Philippians 4:4) Speak to people and be friendly. My daughter Joy said to me, "Mom, you always feel the college is so friendly, and they are. But, Mom, do you know why you see that wherever you go? It's because you're always friendly first."

If her words are true, great, but I truly work on being friendly all the time. No, I'm not where I want to be. If someone pays you a compliment and you don't feel you deserve that compliment, why don't you become what they think you are?

- Pay compliments often. Praise is a reinforcement of good.
- Call people on the phone and leave uplifting and kind messages.
- Write notes of encouragement and praise often. It pumps life into people.
- Find the good in people and tell them before it's too late. Express it now—not when they are in the casket.

Be a spirit setter and find the joys in life.
God has definitely let me see sunshine on some very cloudy days. The day I was diagnosed with incurable kidney disease, my personality started to change. I became so consumed with what I could not change that I almost became down and depressed.

My husband asked me a strange question as we were on our drive to Mayo Clinic to get some added help. "Hey," he said, "have you seen my wife lately?"

I thought, "I think he's flipped. I'm right here, and I'm his wife." I immediately said, "You know I'm your wife! What do you mean?"

He said, "No, my wife is upbeat and full of life. She would not let this blow knock her down. She would remain upbeat."

His words slapped me right in the face. When we arrived at Mayo Clinic and while we were waiting to be called for my appointment, I asked my husband if he'd listen for my name. He agreed, and I left.

By this time, I didn't want to have any part of this pity part in my life. I went outside and found a Shakey's Pizza Parlor hat and a stick. I decided to become the elevator operator that Mayo Clinic did not have. I started inviting people to ride my elevator, and I had the privilege of pushing all the buttons. On my elevator, I greeted every rider with a smile and an encouraging word, and we had a ball. We started singing, laughing, and before I knew it, the word spread. People were waiting to ride with me.

I got so excited and involved in people's lives that I forgot I was very ill and that I would possibly be on kidney dialysis by age 40. Well, I am here to tell you that I'll be 61 on July 23, 2007, and I'm alive and doing just fine! Yes, I still have a kidney damage, and now my liver enzymes are affected, but I'm still fine. I have a great doctor here in the local area, Dr. David Ashbach, and a great doctor at Mayo Clinic, Dr. Vincente Torres. I trust them both, and I'm very diligent to have normal checkups. But the Great Physician has allowed me to have a wonderful, fruitful life, and He is totally in control of my life span.

Yes, there are some cloudy days, but I choose to live above the clouds and try to bring sunshine to all who cross my path.

The "Kissing Couple," Roy and JoJo, at Epcot Disney World 2006

Afterword

I wondered as I wrote this final page, "How can I sum it all up?" Yes, we all can have even more joy through the ups and downs of life—it is up to us. The hard times will come; I promise. Even as I finish writing this book, I am facing the heaviest of obstacles. A week ago my husband Roy had nine biopsies on his prostate gland, and yesterday, the phone call came.

The doctor left a message on our answering machine that went something like this, "Mr. Moffitt, this is Dr. Unni, and I'm calling about your biopsy results. There are some areas of concern that we would like to discuss with you face to face. We would also like to schedule an appointment to discuss your options." My heart again was hit with heartache and sadness as we learned that my husband Roy has prostate cancer. I immediately thought of several of the following ways I try to utilize to live above the down times.

1. I smile through the tears. Someone needs me today. A smile is contagious; we should pass it on.
2. I try to leave my world and enter the world of others.
3. I try to look for the needs of others, and then I try to go one step further and meet those needs.
4. I try to build people. I never want to be guilty of breaking a person. I always want to look for the good in people.
5. I want to love people—before it is too late.
6. When a need arises, I do not say, "What's in it for me?" I instead try to say, "What can I do to help?"

7. I can be a burden, or I can bear a burden.
8. I can hurt people, or I can help people. The choice is mine.
9. I can sing, pray, and rejoice—all three uplift my spirit and in turn the spirits of those with whom I come in contact.
10. I cry out to God to meet my every need. He can take my painfulness when others cannot. He loves me, and He truly is the only One Who can help me through the down times.
11. I trust God; He has the only answers. *"Trust in the LORD with all thine heart; and lean not unto thine own understanding. In all thy ways acknowledge him, and he shall direct thy paths. Be not wise in thine own eyes: fear the LORD, and depart from evil."* (Proverbs 3:5-7)

Yes, life is like a carousel. I do not want to ride the horse that is stationary, sits still, and does nothing. I want to choose the horse that goes up and down. Sure, it will have breakdowns, disappointments, and reversals, but, oh, what fun! Life is truly a merry-go-round. I plan to stay on my horse until the end of the ride. I trust that I will be able to say that we will all live together happily ever after.

The End...
No! The Beginning!